World War One

An illustrated
History in colour
1914-1918

Robert Hoare
Edited by R J Unstead

Special Adviser:
Dr J M Roberts
Fellow and Tutor in Modern History
at Merton College, Oxford

Macdonald Educational

First published 1973
Reprinted 1974

© Macdonald and Company
(Publishers) Limited
49-50 Poland Street
London W1A 2LG

ISBN 0 356 04091 7

Library of Congress
Catalog Card Number
72-92427

Planning and Co-ordination :
Sue Jacquemier
Research : Bridget Hadaway

Printed in Great Britain by :
Morrison and Gibb Ltd
London and Edinburgh

Cover illustration: HMS Lion in action at
Jutland. Painted by W. Wyllie RA.
Back cover illustration: from a recruiting
poster for the U.S. Army.
Below: German soldiers in a counterattack.

Contents

Introduction

The Years of Slaughter

World War One was worse than any previous war in history. In it, more people died and more damage was done than ever before in an international conflict. The slaughter was appalling, particularly among foot soldiers. The casualties of the whole war totalled more than 20 million.

Death came in brutal forms. Men were mown down by machine guns, blown to pieces by explosive shells, died in torpedoed merchant ships and in open boats on the Atlantic, were crushed under the tracks of the fearsome new tanks. Some died futilely, drowned in the mud of the battlefields. Some died horribly "If you want to find the old battalion, I know where they are," said one war song, "Hanging on the old barbed wire."

The war took its toll of the civil population too. Air-raids caused little damage, but as each side tried to starve the other, millions, weakened by years of under-feeding, fell victims to disease.

At first the war was a brave challenge to gallant young men. But by 1918 the war held little glamour for either side. It was a cruel, bitter struggle. Yet to the end there remained one shred of solace for people mercifully unable to see into the future. At least their sufferings would benefit humanity, for they thought this was the war to end all wars . . .

Assassination at Sarajevo

On a hot summer's morning in June 1914, 19-year-old Gavrilo Princip fired two shots in a street in Sarajevo, Bosnia. They killed the Archduke Franz Ferdinand of Austria-Hungary and his wife and started a series of events which led to World War I.

Princip was a member of a group of six plotters who travelled to Sarajevo from Serbia, and Austria-Hungary blamed Serbia for what had happened. Backed by Germany, they made many demands of Serbia. Serbia agreed to most of them but not all and, one month after the assassination, on 28 July, Austria-Hungary declared war on Serbia. Next day, Serbia's ally, Russia, began to prepare for war, and the time-table of events afterwards went like this:

31 July Germany warned France not to help Russia if war broke out.

1 August Germany declared war on Russia.

2 August Germany threatened Belgium.

3 August Germany declared war on France.

4 August Germany invaded Belgium. Britain declared war on Germany. World War I had begun*.

▽ The place: Sarajevo, capital of the Austrian province of Bosnia. The date: 28 June. **Archduke Franz Ferdinand** heir to the throne of Austria-Hungary, and his wife, Sophie, are greeted by a local official. The Archduke was in Bosnia to attend army manoeuvres in place of the Emperor Franz Josef. He and the Duchess were driven through Sarajevo in an open motor-car.

*Events leading up to the war are described in more detail on page 52.

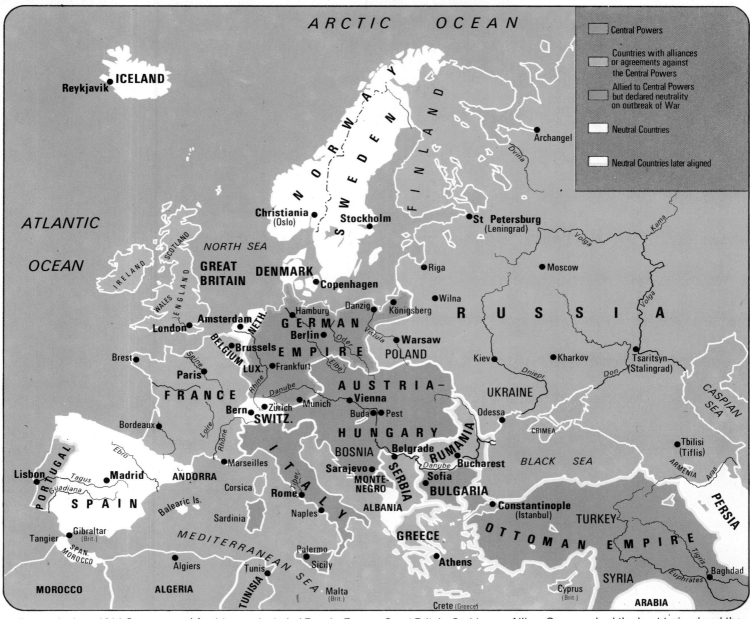

△ **Europe in June 1914** Germany and Austria-Hungary were allies. These Central Powers, as they were called, were later joined by Bulgaria and the Ottoman Empire (present-day Turkey). The countries in opposition to them at first included Russia, France, Great Britain, Serbia, Montenegro and Belgium and they became known as the Allies. Later, Italy, Portugal, Japan, Rumania, Greece and the United States entered the war on the side of the Allies. Germany had the best trained and the best equipped army in the world. But Russia had the greatest number of men available and the British Royal Navy controlled the seas of the world (cf p. 6).

△ **Gavrilo Princip** a student from Belgrade. Born in Bosnia, he hated Austrian rule.

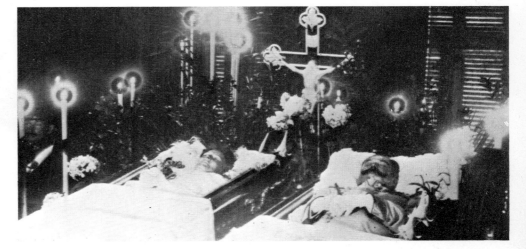

△ **The bodies of Franz Ferdinand and his wife** in the house of the governor in Sarajevo. The funeral took place five days later in Vienna. The first bullet hit the Archduke in the jugular vein. The second hit his wife in the side. "Don't die; live for my children," the dying Archduke told her, but she was already unconscious.

5

Rival Navies

△ **Admiral Alfred P. Friedrich von Tirpitz**
"father of the German Navy", Secretary of State
for the Imperial Navy 1897-1916; appointed Lord
High Admiral 1911. In the war, he commanded the
German Navy from 1914 to March 1916 and
gave orders for the ruthless use of U-boats in
attacks on Allied ships.

△**Admiral Sir John Arbuthnot Fisher**
became First Sea Lord in charge of the
British Royal Navy in 1904. He reorganized
the Navy, moved more ships into the North Sea,
and introduced a revolutionary new battleship,
HMS Dreadnought.

In 1914, the British Royal Navy was the largest in the world. But for 17 years, Germany's navy had been growing. In 1899, Britain had 29 major battleships, Germany 7. In 1914, Britain had 24, Germany 13. The gap between the navies had closed significantly.

For many years before the war, the two countries were engaged in a race to keep pace with each other in the building of battleships. Germany began to build up the Imperial Navy in 1897. The cost in taxes to the German people was high. But the emperor, Kaiser Wilhelm II, and Admiral von Tirpitz told them that a stronger navy was essential to defend the country.

King Edward VII and Admiral Sir John Fisher soon saw the danger to British sea power. As Sea Lord, Fisher scrapped over 150 old ships and, in 1906, produced HMS Dreadnought. This new battleship made every other battleship in the world out of date. She carried ten 12-inch guns and had a speed of 21 knots.

Building battleships was costing both countries great sums of money and there were talks between them to see if they could come to some agreement as to how many ships they built each year. But nothing was agreed and, in 1912, Britain said she would build two major ships for every one built by Germany.

When the war began, Britain still had a bigger navy than Germany's and two new super-dreadnoughts with eight 15-inch guns were nearly completed.

Relative strengths of the British Royal Navy and the German Imperial Navy at the start of the war.

	Britain	Germany
Dreadnoughts	24	13
Battle Cruisers	10	6
Pre-dreadnoughts	38	30
Cruisers	47	14
Light Cruisers	61	35
Destroyers	225	152
Submarines	76	30

▽ The super-dreadnought **Malaya.** Guns: eight
15-inch, fourteen 6-inch. Speed: 25 knots.
These were to be the fastest and most powerful
battleships in the world, and Britain was building
five in 1914.

▷ **SMS Rheinland** one of the first German
dreadnoughts. Displacement: 18,900 tons.
Length: 472 feet. Beam: 89 feet. Guns: Twelve
11-inch, twelve 5·9-inch, sixteen 3·4-inch.
Torpedo tubes: Six 17·7-inch. Speed: 20 knots.
Crew: 963. Armour: 11–11½ inches thick.

△ The French Navy included battleships like the **Gaulois.**

△ Two British battleships **HMS Agamemnon** and **HMS Cornwallis.**

△ **Karl von Müller,** captain of the German raider *Emden.* She sank or captured 25 Allied ships in the Indian Ocean in late 1914. Battered by the Australian cruiser *Sydney* she surrendered on 9 November.

△ **The letter from Captain Glossop** of *HMAS Sydney*, requesting Müller to surrender his ship.

The Western Front

At the start of the war, Kaiser Wilhelm II remarked to General Helmuth von Moltke, the German Commander-in-Chief, "Remember we can be in Paris in a fortnight." In fact, German troops could see the top of the Eiffel Tower by September.

But they got no farther. The Germans entered Belgium on August 4 and swept forward. They were held for a time at Mons by the British. Then the British had to fall back to just north of Paris. Meantime the French had formed up on the River Marne.

Driven back, the Germans turned north to get round the Allied line, but they were held in the bloody Battle of Ypres. Afterwards the opposing armies dug themselves in along a line from the Belgian coast to Switzerland, and this rarely moved more than ten miles either way in the next four years.

Long, bitter battles took place whenever each side launched a major attack, and the numbers of dead, wounded and missing were appalling. In 1916, the French held out for months against a relentless German attack at Verdun, at a cost of almost a third of a million men. Later the Germans resisted a British counter-offensive on the Somme. They lost almost half a million men. But the Allied casualties totalled 623,000.

△ **Troops of the Belgian Army.** They were poorly trained and lacked good equipment.

△ Aftermath of battle: **German prisoners.**

▽ **Machine-gun** in a German dug-out.

△ French Commander-in-Chief, General Joffre (left), President Raymond Poincaré, King George V of Britain, Marshal Foch of France and the British C.-in-C., Lord Haig.

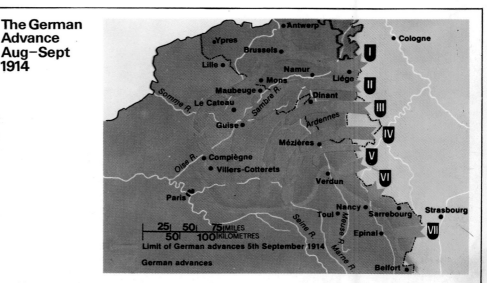

The German Advance Aug–Sept 1914

Limit of German advances 5th September 1914

German advances

△ After sweeping through Belgium, the German armies invaded France. In their march to the Marne, the German Chief of Staff, Moltke, decided to concentrate east of Paris. But the advance was held by French and English forces, and after the battle of the Marne, the Germans were forced to retreat.

△**Over the top.** These British soldiers are backing up the assault wave ahead of them. Overladen with small arms, ammunition, hand grenades and rations they walk into no man's land "without any fuss," in the words of one officer. Yet, at any moment, they may face a hail of enemy fire.

▽The German offensive of 1916 was aimed at the French fortress of **Verdun.** The battle that followed produced the most appalling losses of the war. It went on for five months, but General Pétain declared "Ils ne passeront pas" (They shall not pass).

△**French soldier wearing gas-mask.** Poison gas was first used by the Germans in the second Battle of Ypres in April/May 1915. This was contrary to their promise made at the Hague Convention in 1907.

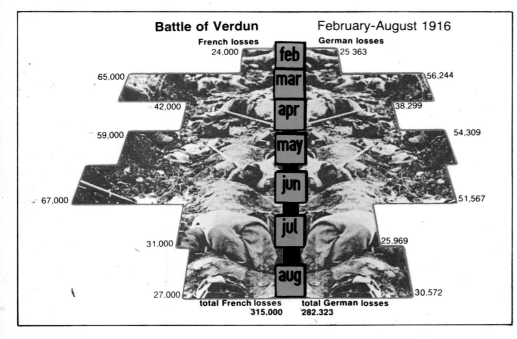

Battle of Verdun   February-August 1916

French losses		German losses
24,000	feb	25 363
65,000	mar	56,244
42,000	apr	38,299
59,000	may	54,309
67,000	jun	51,567
31,000	jul	25,969
27,000	aug	30,572

total French losses **315,000**   total German losses **282,323**

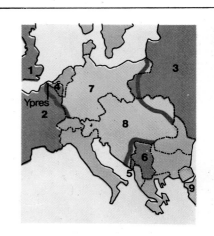

△This map of Europe shows the lines of **the three battle fronts** at the end of 1914.

Allied Powers
1 Great Britain
2 France
3 Russia
4 Belgium
5 Montenegro
6 Serbia

Central Powers
7 Germany
8 Austria-Hungary
9 Turkey

Already the losses had been tremendous. In the first Battle of Ypres, the British had lost over 50,000 men. Worse was to come.

△Heavy artillery like this **British howitzer** was used to bombard areas before attacks.

The Horror of the Trenches

"We have just come out of a place so terrible that a raving lunatic could never imagine the horror." An officer wrote these words after two weeks in the front line during an Allied attack. He was writing about life in the trenches.

In 1914, troops on the Western Front dug ditches and sheltered in them from enemy fire. Later they made these into deeper and wider trenches. Second and third lines of trenches were dug, with others connecting these lines. In front of the first trenches were laid tangled masses of barbed wire. Beyond lay No Man's Land, a stretch of open ground pitted with craters left by exploding shells.

In an attack, the enemy lines were subjected to heavy artillery bombardment before the troops went over the top. But, far from being wiped out, the enemy was still able to deliver a murderous fire at the advancing infantry. Sometimes, a few hundred yards of trenches were captured, but counterattacks could be launched from further back and the stalemate was resumed.

FIELD-MARSHAL SIR DOUGLAS HAIG

△ **Haig** took over from Sir John French as British Commander-in-Chief in 1915. He was unshakeably confident that the Allies would win the war.

△ **General Erich von Ludendorff** was in command of the German Army from 1916.

▷ An artist's impression of the horrors of **war on the Western Front.** The explosion of millions of shells from heavy artillery pitted the ground with craters. Drainage was totally destroyed and rain turned the earth into a sea of slimy mud where men could drown in the water-filled craters. In the picture, the surviving soldiers are sheltering from the threat of enemy fire and the artist has added the ultimate horror—poison gas.

△ This aerial photograph was taken by an early reconnaissance aircraft. It shows a **German trench system.** Information of this kind was vital to the success of an attack and aircraft were increasingly used to obtain it.

△**Allied troops** advance upon an enemy position under cover of a heavy barrage from artillery behind them. The barrage would stop when the troops neared the enemy.

△ Tommies going over the top in the **Battle of the Somme.** A way had been cut through their own barbed wire but thousands died because the German wire had not been destroyed by bombardment.

The Sinking of the Lusitania

On May 1, 1915, as, in a drizzle of rain, the Lusitania, one of the most splendid ocean liners in the world, prepared to sail from New York, an American millionaire, Alfred Vanderbilt, declared: "The Germans dare not sink this ship!"

Vanderbilt was speaking to some reporters. They had come aboard because they had read a warning in the newspapers that morning. The warning was from the German Embassy. It said that ships of any kind sailing into the sea around Britain were in danger of attack.

Six days later the *Lusitania*, close to the south coast of Ireland, received messages that U-boats were operating nearby. Meantime Kapitan-leutnant Walther Schweiger was ordering the crew of the U20 to dive. Minutes later he had his periscope lined up on the *Lusitania* and a torpedo was streaking towards the ship. She went down ten miles off the Old Head of Kinsale, her wireless tapping out *SOS*. From Ireland, ships hurried to the scene but 1,198 people drowned including 124 Americans. Among them was Alfred Vanderbilt. Although he could not swim, he gave his life-jacket to a young woman.

△ **Before the *Lusitania* sailed.** These women have heard of the German warning in the morning's newspapers but, like everyone else aboard, they are not worried.

▽ **Top: A German submarine** or *unterseeboot,* the U9. She sank three British cruisers in the North Sea two months after the start of the war, causing a loss of 1,459 men. **Bottom: Loading ammunition for deck guns.** U-boats obtained supplies from ships at sea.

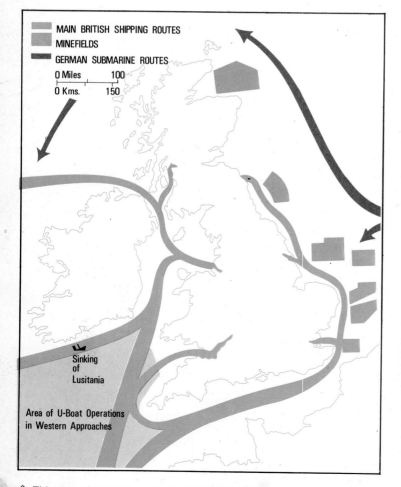

MAIN BRITISH SHIPPING ROUTES
MINEFIELDS
GERMAN SUBMARINE ROUTES

0 Miles — 100
0 Kms. — 150

Sinking of Lusitania

Area of U-Boat Operations in Western Approaches

△ This map shows **the routes taken by Allied ships,** the routes followed by German U-boats to avoid the British mine-fields, and where the *Lusitania* went down, 10 miles off the Irish coast.

Twenty minutes after the torpedo struck her, the *Lusitania* went down by the bow. In Germany, newspapers described her sinking as "an extraordinary success", and claimed that the ship was carrying arms. Allied newspapers condemned the attack on "innocent and defenceless people". The President of the United States sent a note of protest to the Kaiser. But U-boats went on sinking unarmed vessels, including a number of American cargo ships. On April 2, 1917, President Wilson declared war on Germany. Posters were put up all over the United States calling for men to join the armed forces. They said: "Remember the *Lusitania*".

Guns

Artillery and machine-guns played an important part in the fighting on all fronts. In the pattern of trench warfare such as was fought on the Western Front, an intense bombardment of enemy positions by artillery preceded an attack by infantry.

In the Battle of the Somme in July-November 1916, 900 heavy and 1,100 light guns were massed on a front ten miles long, and two million shells were fired. The gunfire was heard on Hampstead Heath in London, nearly 300 miles away. Artillery used two kinds of shells: high explosive—thick steel casing, heavy charge—for use against stone, concrete, barbed wire; and shrapnel—thin casing, weak charge, filled with lead pellets—for use against men. Some machine-guns had greater fire-power than a company of riflemen. A single machine-gun nest could exact a grim toll of infantry.

△ **September 1917.** These French soldiers have just moved into a newly-won position and are setting up a heavy mortar.

▷ **French Hotchkiss 8-mm machine-gun,** 1914 model. Air-cooled and light, this gun was used by the British as well as the French. The use of machine-guns from defensive positions became a significant feature of fighting on the Western Front.

△ **A massive German howitzer.** By the end of the war, German guns called *Big Berthas* were firing shells on Paris from 76 miles away.

▷ **British 15-inch Howitzer Mark 1.** Range: 10,000 yards. Weight of shell: 1,450 lb. Crew: 12. Winston Churchill, First Lord of the Admiralty, ordered twelve of these big guns in 1914 and they were sent into action in France manned by members of the Royal Marine Howitzer Brigade. Howitzers have short barrels in relation to the size of their shells. They fired shells in a high arc and were used against stationary targets beyond obstacles.

▷ **United States 4.7-inch field gun M 1906.**
Range: 7,490 yards. Weight with limber:
3 tons 18 cwt. Muzzle velocity: 1,700 feet per
second. Weight of shell: 60 lb. Crew: 6–8.
Traverse: 4 degrees left and right. Artillery of
this kind can be towed into action positions
with relative speed in order to support
infantry or armoured forces.

▽ **French 75-mm field gun,** known as the
"miracle" gun because it was so much
better than other artillery at the war's start.
Better for accuracy, mobility, range and rate
of fire (6 rounds per minute normally), it has
a buffer recoil system allowing the crew to
fire repeatedly without laying the gun on
target each time.

▷ **Russian 15-cm field gun,** an 1884 model. In
1914, Russian industry was nowhere near as
advanced as that in Britain and France. Small
arms and machine-guns were being made in
some quantities, but for their artillery the
Russians depended on models bought from
other countries which were anything but
up-to-date. The Russian army was ill-
organized, poorly equipped and often
badly shod.

Tanks

In the Battle of the Somme on September 15, 1916, German infantry saw a frightening sight. Lumbering towards them across

No Man's Land were 24 metal monsters moving on tracks. They were the first tanks to be used in the history of warfare. The tank was a secret weapon developed in Britain through the efforts of Winston Churchill. Haig made the decision to use the tank while other British leaders hesitated. In the event, most of the tanks broke down. But a year later, on November 20, 1917, 476 tanks went into action at Cambrai and won what might have been a decisive victory. 8,000 prisoners were taken and over 100 guns captured but there were insufficient reserves to follow up the advantage.

▽ **British Mark IV.** Guns: six .303-in. Lewis. Crew: 8. Speed: 3.7 m.p.h. Weight: 26 tons. The bundle of wood called a fascine would be dropped in a ditch to help the tank to get across to the other side.

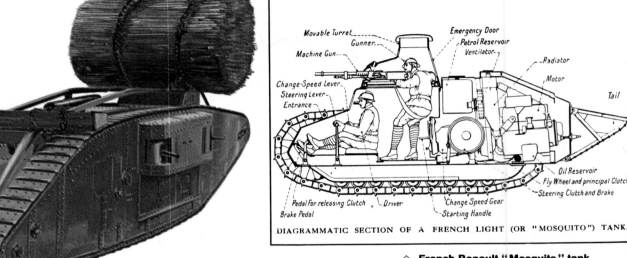

DIAGRAMMATIC SECTION OF A FRENCH LIGHT (OR "MOSQUITO") TANK.

△ **French Renault "Mosquito" tank,** equivalent to the British Whippet. Not quite so good at crossing rough country, it had a good turn of speed. Both were classed light tanks.

△ **A German Albatros DV fighter** dives to strafe an Allied tank engulfed in fire from a flame-thrower. In the spring offensive of 1918, the Germans used ground-air co-operation of this kind. Yet this incident seems unlikely to have happened. As the photo comes from a German source, perhaps it was a mock-up used for training purposes.

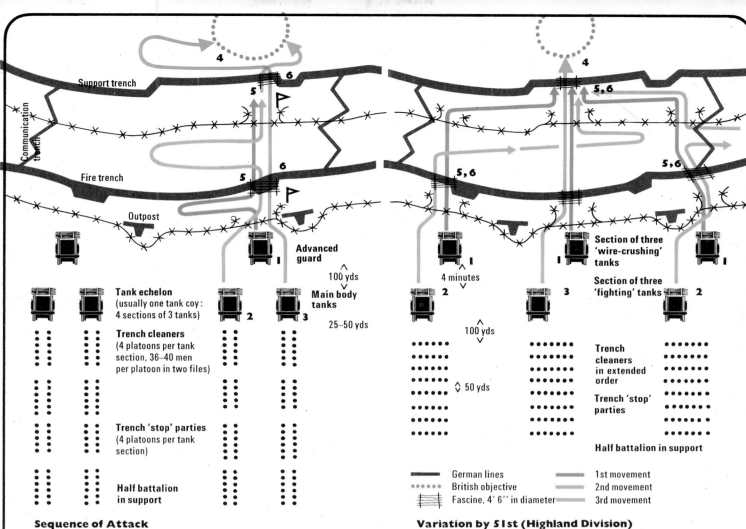

Support trench

Communication trench

Fire trench

Outpost

Advanced guard

Tank echelon
(usually one tank coy: 4 sections of 3 tanks)

Main body tanks

100 yds

25–50 yds

Trench cleaners
(4 platoons per tank section, 36–40 men per platoon in two files)

Trench 'stop' parties
(4 platoons per tank section)

Half battalion in support

4 minutes

100 yds

50 yds

Section of three 'wire-crushing' tanks

Section of three 'fighting' tanks

Trench cleaners in extended order

Trench 'stop' parties

Half battalion in support

——— German lines	——— 1st movement
······ British objective	——— 2nd movement
Fascine, 4' 6'' in diameter	——— 3rd movement

Sequence of Attack

1 Advanced guard tanks crush wire, create gap and swing left to rake fire trench with main and secondary armament.
2 These are followed by second tank in each section, which drops fascine, plants flag and crosses fire trench, then swings left to rake support trench.
3 The last tank in each section crushes second wire barrier, drops fascine, plants flag and crosses the support trench towards the objective.
4 All tanks then rally in the vicinity of the objective.
5 Infantry 'trench cleaners' then clear the German lines (2 platoons per trench) from right to left, aided by 2nd & 3rd tanks.
6 Infantry 'stop' platoons secure trenches, set up blocks and improve wire gaps, through which the reserves then pass.

Variation by 51st (Highland Division)

1 'Wire-crushing' tanks dispose of advanced posts, break wire, cross trench (with aid of fascine) and drive on to breach second wire belt.
2 Two flanking fighting tanks cross fascine bridges, then turn right to shoot up the fire trench.
3 The remaining fighting tank passes straight ahead to bridge support trench.
4 General tank rally.
5,6 Infantry, deployed in extended order, carry out normal 'cleaning' and 'stopping' rôle (from left to right).

△ **Diagram of tank battle drill** invented by Lt.-Col. (later Maj.-Gen.) John Frederick Charles Fuller. He believed tanks had a vital part in warfare and is today remembered as one of the most brilliant military thinkers of the century.

▽ **The Anglo-American Mark VIII heavy tank,** the International. Four of these tanks had been finished by the end of the war in 1918. Weighing 37 tons, they were the heaviest tank to be produced in the war. Crew: 8. Armament: two 23-calibre 6-pdrs with 208 rounds and seven .3-inch Browning machine guns with 13,484 rounds.

The Turkish Empire

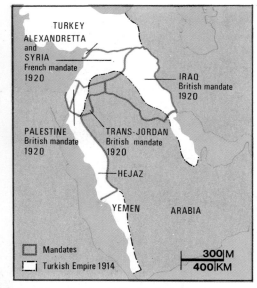

This map shows the **Turkish Empire** as it was in 1914 and what happened to it at the end of the war.

Map labels:
- TURKEY
- ALEXANDRETTA and SYRIA French mandate 1920
- IRAQ British mandate 1920
- PALESTINE British mandate 1920
- TRANS-JORDAN British mandate 1920
- HEJAZ
- YEMEN
- ARABIA
- Mandates
- Turkish Empire 1914
- 300 M / 400 KM

In 1914, Turkey was part of the Ottoman Empire ruled by the Sultan Mohammed V. She was known as "the sick man of Europe" because the empire was gradually dwindling away as her countries became independent or were annexed by major powers.

By 1913, the Ottoman Empire had no land in Europe but Turkey itself. She began to reorganize her army with the help of General Liman von Sanders from Germany.

Since 1908, the Young Turks had been in power, and the Sultan had little influence over them. When war broke out, they agreed secretly to help Germany.

Two dreadnoughts were being built in England for Turkey and she still hoped to collect them. But Britain took over the battleships and offered to give back the money Turkey had paid for them. Turkey protested about this.

Then, on August 10 a German battle-cruiser and cruiser escaped from the British by slipping into a Turkish port. Next day, Turkey said she had bought them and to prove it the German crews started wearing red fezes!

For two months Turkey kept out of the war officially. Then, on October 29, Turkish warships helped the Germans to bombard Russian ports on the Black Sea, and the Allies declared war on Turkey.

The Young Turks had decided to take a risky gamble. They hoped, if the Central Powers won the war, to regain part of their lost empire.

These **Turkish infantrymen** are reasonably well equipped. But in 1914 many of Turkey's troops were badly dressed, half-starved and short of supplies. Some of them had to go barefoot. But they were brave fighters.

△ **The heir to the Turkish throne** (astrakhan hat) with officers of the army. A writer of the time said of the army: "Other armies may give way to privation and untended sickness but that of the Sultan will go forward as long as it can stand."

▷ **This modern cartoon** shows Turkey in the form of a tired-looking woman being carried to war along with the Sultan, Mohammed V, by a group of Young Turks including Enver Pasha, Minister of War. The figure in grey on the left is a German General urging them on.

The Dardanelles Disaster

△ **The green square** covers the entrance to the Dardanelles leading to the heavily-fortified Narrows. In February-March, 1915 an Allied fleet bombarded Turkish gun positions on the Dardanelles and, on March 18, 18 battleships tried to force their way through the strait. Three were sunk, three crippled, 700 men being lost. The fleet withdrew.

▽ **In the attack on the Dardanelles** on March 18, 1915, success seemed at hand as the Allied fleet steamed towards the Narrows. Then from this battleship, the French *Bouvet,* there came an explosion and she sank with all hands in two minutes. She had run into an undetected minefield barring the way.

The Dardanelles is a narrow strait joining the Aegean Sea with the Sea of Marmara and separating Turkey in Europe from Turkey in Asia. In 1915, the Dardanelles held great importance for the Allies and they wanted to gain control of the strait.

If they could do this, they would open a route to supply Russia with desperately-needed munitions, would knock Turkey out of the war and be able to attack Austria through the Balkans.

Unfortunately, Kitchener did not feel able to release troops in large numbers from the Western Front, but Churchill pressed so hard for his cherished plan that the Cabinet agreed to make it a naval operation. In February 1915, warships began bombarding the Dardanelles shore defences but, without troops and minesweepers, these attacks merely gave the Turks time to organize defence.

On April 25, an Allied force of British, Australian, New Zealand and French troops under General Hamilton landed on the beaches of the Gallipoli peninsula. They fought heroically but all surprise had been lost. The Turks resisted with desperate courage and, instead of a swift Allied advance on Constantinople, there developed a bloody slogging match with the stalemate of trench warfare.

During the hot summer, sickness gravely weakened the Allied forces and, by November, it was decided to abandon the whole enterprise. General Birdwood carried out a brilliant withdrawal, but nearly a quarter of a million men had been killed, wounded or evacuated sick. The Turks also suffered heavy losses and were in fact so near to collapse that if fresh Allied forces had been sent, success might still have been achieved. As it was, over-optimism and muddle turned a brilliant plan into a disaster that prolonged the war.

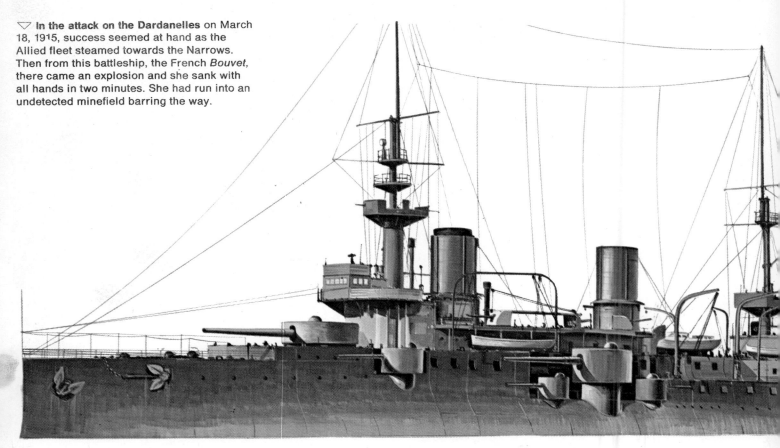

△ **An old fortress** called Seddulbahir on the Dardanelles.

△ **Old, short of ammunition and small in calibre, the Turkish guns** defending the beaches at Gallipoli were no threat to the Allied landings. They were supported in some places by dummy batteries of small guns firing only powder to draw the enemy fire.

△ **Troops pushing a gun ashore at Anzac Cove.** In the attack of April 25, 1915, the invaders met a storm of fire on some beaches. Others faced less resistance. But one Anzac said afterwards "To get at the bloody Turk was all we cared."

△ **Troops from Australia and New Zealand** in the fighting at Gallipoli which provided them with their first experience of battle. The Anzacs, as they were nicknamed, soon won a reputation for bravery and sportsmanship. In the first days at Gallipoli, some young Anzacs offered £5 for the chance of going "over the top."

The Cost of being Neutral

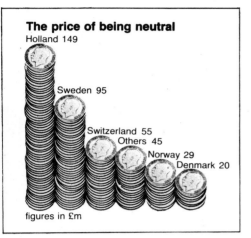

The price of being neutral

Holland 149

Sweden 95

Switzerland 55
Others 45

Norway 29 Denmark 20

figures in £m

△ **Neutrality did not save a nation** from suffering some of the consequences of war. This chart indicates what those consequences were in terms of hard cash. The cost shown here is made up of the loss in trade and the amount spent on keeping military forces in a state of readiness. Holland's dependence on sea trade is emphasised by the position that she occupies in this chart.

▽ **A neutral ship struck by a torpedo** from a German U-boat. The Allied shipping blockade was irksome to the neutrals. They resented having cargoes confiscated as contraband. But they liked the Germans no more. From the war's start, neutral ships were at risk from U-boats and after February 1, 1917, when Germany declared unrestricted U-boat warfare, every neutral ship on the high seas was in danger.

Sooner or later, all the major powers of the world and many of the smaller nations became involved in the war. However, two dozen countries managed to remain neutral. These included Holland, Norway, Sweden, Denmark, Spain and Switzerland.

The impact of the war was felt by all of the neutrals to a greater or lesser degree. Britain controlled the seas and, from the start, set up a blockade to prevent Germany obtaining supplies. Lists were produced of goods considered to be contraband. Neutral ships could be stopped by the Allies and if they were carrying contraband it would be confiscated.

In November 1914, Britain declared the North Sea a war zone in which all ships would be exposed to mines and other hazards. Neutral ships were forced to follow routes on which ships of the Royal Navy were waiting to inspect their cargoes. There was also the threat to neutral shipping from Germany's U-boats. Much bargaining went on between Britain and the sea-trading neutrals. For example, she allowed Denmark to import coal and oil from Germany as well as from Britain.

At the same time, Denmark was importing nitrogen fodders from America and neither the British blockade nor the German U-boats interfered with this trade.

Neutral Switzerland, lying landlocked between France and Germany, needed coal and iron from Germany, and foodstuffs brought part of the way by sea. From the Swiss, both warring sides wanted watches and other precision instruments which the Swiss were particularly skilled at making. As a result, both of them came to agreements with Switzerland.

The Red Cross

The Red Cross was founded by a Swiss, Henri Dunant, and the headquarters of the International Committee of the Red Cross were in Geneva, Switzerland. The Swiss and the Red Cross helped hordes of destitute people driven out of enemy countries at the war's start. They helped to exchange men caught in enemy countries. The Red Cross helped to trace people cut off from their families, passed on information about prisoners-of-war, and sent on letters from prisoners on both sides—often half a million a day.

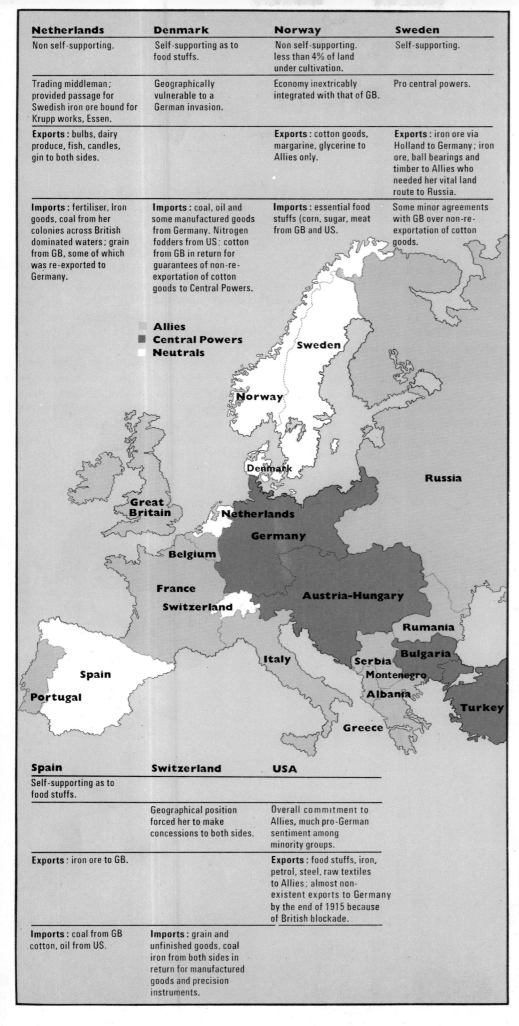

	Netherlands	Denmark	Norway	Sweden
	Non self-supporting.	Self-supporting as to food stuffs.	Non self-supporting. less than 4% of land under cultivation.	Self-supporting.
	Trading middleman; provided passage for Swedish iron ore bound for Krupp works, Essen.	Geographically vulnerable to a German invasion.	Economy inextricably integrated with that of GB.	Pro central powers.
Exports	bulbs, dairy produce, fish, candles, gin to both sides.		cotton goods, margarine, glycerine to Allies only.	iron ore via Holland to Germany; iron ore, ball bearings and timber to Allies who needed her vital land route to Russia.
Imports	fertiliser, Iron goods, coal from her colonies across British dominated waters; grain from GB, some of which was re-exported to Germany.	coal, oil and some manufactured goods from Germany. Nitrogen fodders from US; cotton from GB in return for guarantees of non-re-exportation of cotton goods to Central Powers.	essential food stuffs (corn, sugar, meat from GB and US.	Some minor agreements with GB over non-re-exportation of cotton goods.

Allies
Central Powers
Neutrals

	Spain	Switzerland	USA
	Self-supporting as to food stuffs.		
		Geographical position forced her to make concessions to both sides.	Overall commitment to Allies, much pro-German sentiment among minority groups.
Exports	iron ore to GB.		food stuffs, iron, petrol, steel, raw textiles to Allies; almost non-existent exports to Germany by the end of 1915 because of British blockade.
Imports	coal from GB cotton, oil from US.	grain and unfinished goods, coal iron from both sides in return for manufactured goods and precision instruments.	

◁ This chart summarises the position of **the main neutral countries** (including the United States up to 1917) during World War One. The needs of the Allies and the Central Powers and the neutrals themselves were inextricable. This led to compromises by both warring sides.

△ **Although Belgians were officially neutral,** civilian snipers like these caused some trouble to the German armies in 1914 as they swept swiftly across Belgium.

△ **Drowned mother and child,** victims of a German U-boat. This wartime enlistment poster from America gives a reminder of the cruelties of the war at sea.

Birth of the Fighter

In August 1914, France had about 1,500 military aircraft, Germany 1,000 and Britain 179. It was the first time aeroplanes had played a part in a war.

At first, they were used only for observing the enemy. But as pilots encountered enemy aircraft they began to throw things at them. One German threw a brick! Next the pilots began to take up pistols and rifles and shoot at the enemy pilots and from this it was a short step to fitting machine-guns in the aeroplanes: thus the fighter plane was born.

At this time, two types of aircraft were in use—the pusher, with its propeller at the back, and the tractor, with its propeller at the front. The pusher was more suitable for the use of a machine-gun because its propeller did not hamper the gunner firing forwards. But the pusher was slower and less manoeuvrable than the tractor. In July 1915, the Germans produced the first forward-firing tractor fighter, the Fokker E 1, and it gave them command in the air. Later the Allies produced similar machines and from then on aerial combat increased. The most successful pilots became popular heroes known as aces. Immelman and Boelcke were the first. Guynemer, Ball and von Richthofen came later (*cf* p. 56).

△ **Anthony Fokker,** a Dutch aircraft designer. His Fokker E 1 allowed the machine-gun to fire between the propeller blades.

▷ **One of France's aircraft at the outbreak of the war: the Bleriot XI.** Wing span: 33 ft. 11 in. Length: 27 ft. 10 in. Speed: 66 m.p.h. Normal duration of flight: 3½ hr. In 1913, one of these monoplanes set a record by flying 487 miles.

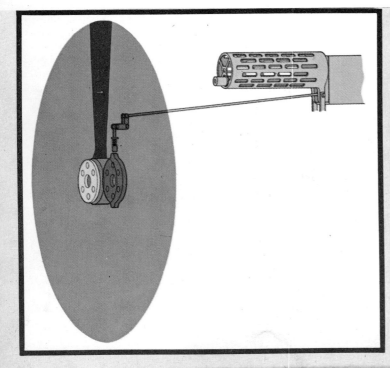

◁ **Anthony Fokker's equipment** that changed the war in the air. The cam aligned with the propeller blade made the gun fire so that the bullet always entered a clear space as it passed through the propeller arc. The E 1 was nicknamed the Fokker Scourge. Its success caused questions to be asked in the British Parliament and led to production of the Sopwith 1½-Strutter.

Details of the Fokker Eindecker (monoplane) which dominated the skies over France in 1915-16. **1** Oberursel U 1 100 h.p. rotary engine. **2** Wooden propeller. **3** Forward fuel tank. **4** *Bungee* rubber cord undercarriage suspension bar. **5** Primer pump. **6** Main undercarriage structure; anchorage point for main flying wires. **7** Wire-spoked wheels. **8** Built-up ribs. **9** Main spars. **10** Leather torsion strips. **11** Rear of undercarriage structure with pulleys for wing-warping wires. **12** Wicker-work pilot's seat. **13** Fuselage bracing wires. **14** Wooden fin and elevator with no fixed surfaces. **15** Tail skid, sprung with *bungee* rubber. **16** Welded steel tube fuselage structure. **17** Doped linen covering. **18** Rear fuel tank. **19** Pylon for landing wires. **20** 7.92 mm. LMG 08/15 synchronised machine-gun.

▽**Unarmed German Albatros biplane** taking off from an airfield in France early in the war. Before the war, this type of aircraft held the world record for length of flight (24 hr. 10 min.).

25

Bombers and Zeppelins

At the start of the war, Germany had the only long-range aircraft in the world. They were rigid airships called zeppelins. Used on the Western Front for bombing, they were not a success.

▽ **A night raider picked out by searchlights.** "It looked like a bar of polished steel," said a special constable watching below. By the end of 1916, 17,340 officers and men were in the anti-aircraft service in Britain and there were twelve squadrons of the Royal Flying Corps with 110 aeroplanes and 2,000 officers and men. Lt. W. Leefe Robinson, first to bring down a "zepp" on British soil, got £4,250 in prizes and the V.C.

When flying low, they were easily brought down by ground fire. But it was hoped that they would spread terror in Britain by bombing big cities. The first attack was made on January 19, 1915, and on May 31 London was raided. England's air defences were speedily improved. In 1916, the first zeppelin was shot down at night by a British fighter, and seven others were destroyed. After this, the Germans used bombers called Gothas. Single-engined aeroplanes could carry only a small bombload; so both sides turned their attention to producing multi-engined bombers.

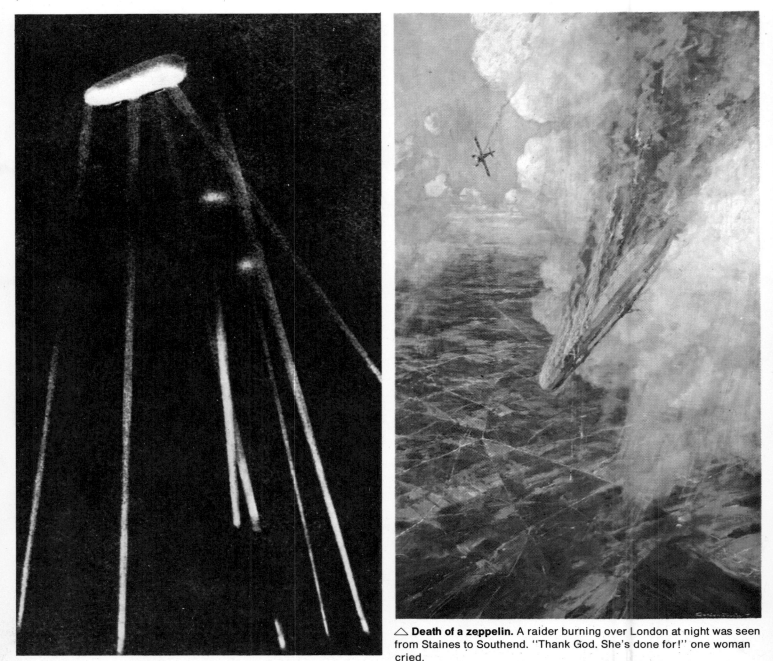

△ **Death of a zeppelin.** A raider burning over London at night was seen from Staines to Southend. "Thank God. She's done for!" one woman cried.

△ **An early bomber: the Short folder seaplane.**
Length: 39 ft. Span: 67 ft. Engine: Gnome
rotary 160-h.p. Speed: 78 m.p.h. Armament:
Bombs or one 14-in. torpedo. Duration: 5 hr.
The wings folded for stowing on ships.

△ **Zeppelin L 14.** Length: 536½ ft. Volume: 1,126,400 cubic ft. Ceiling:
10,000 ft. Endurance: 60 hr. Top speed: 55 m.p.h. Crew: 18. Engines:
four 220-h.p. Zeppelins crossed the English coast 202 times in the war
and dropped 205 tons of bombs, killing 556 people and injuring 1,358.

◁ **Handley Page
V/1500 bomber.**
Three were ready
to attack Berlin
when the war
ended. Length:
64 ft. Wingspan:
128 ft. Engines:
four Rolls-Royce
"Eagles" 350 h.p.
Bomb load: Over
2 tons. Flying
range: Over 1,100
miles.

▽ **German flyer showing early bombing technique.** Two-seaters like
this dropped small bombs on tactical targets such as supply dumps,
airfields and other places near the line. The first real bomber put into
service was the Handley Page 0/100 used to bomb Zeebrugge in 1915.

The Battle of Jutland

On May 30, 1916, the main body of the British Grand Fleet sailed out of Scapa Flow, Scotland, under the command of Admiral Sir John Jellicoe. At the same time, a smaller squadron and the Battle-Cruiser Fleet under Admiral Beatty left other ports.

△ **Admiral Scheer:** he was almost caught in his own trap.

Since 1914, apart from minor engagements, both navies had played a waiting game. The German fleet stayed behind its protective minefields, while the British kept watch, hoping that the enemy would put to sea. Neither commander dared take risks and Jellicoe was "the one man who could lose the war in an afternoon."

In 1916, the German admiral, Scheer, prepared a trap. He sent Admiral Hipper to sea to lure British units towards the main German fleet and, on May 30, Beatty's force of battle-cruisers met Hipper off Jutland, Denmark. The British cruisers suffered badly but Hipper turned away towards Scheer as Jellicoe approached at speed with the Grand Fleet in six columns. Realising that he was outnumbered, Scheer retired behind a smoke-screen and Jellicoe, fearing torpedo attacks at night, did not pursue him.

The Germans regained the shelter of their minefields and the opportunity which Jellicoe longed for had gone. To the Germans, Jutland (or Skaggerak) was a victory; they had sunk 14 ships to eleven, but they never ventured to sea in strength again.

▷ **This map shows the movements of the two fleets** to their fateful rendezvous on Jutland Bank. First contact was made at 14.20 when Vice-Admiral Beatty, with a small group of battle-cruisers, opened fire on a similar group of German ships led by Admiral Franz von Hipper. Each group sought to lead the other towards its main fleet and the fleets made contact at 18.51. This is how they were made up:

	British	German
Battleships	28	22
Battle-cruisers	9	5
Armoured cruisers	8	0
Light cruisers	26	11
Destroyers etc.	80	61

But the battle between these main fleets lasted only five minutes. Scheer turned away, releasing torpedoes and Jellicoe also turned to avoid them.

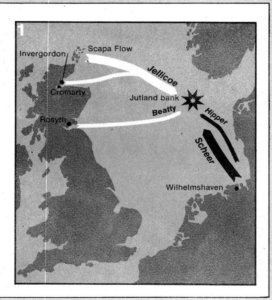

▷ **A line of British warships,** seemingly invulnerable. But against ships of the same size, they perished in minutes. Beatty soon lost two battle-cruisers and said, "There seems to be something wrong with our bloody ships today."

Scheer's fleet came into sight again at 19.12 (twelve minutes past seven at night), and the British opened fire. Within minutes the Germans vanished into the darkness and Jellicoe did not follow. The result was a great disappointment to Britain. Her ships proved inferior in armour and guns, and her only consolation was that the Germans had retreated and never risked another battle.

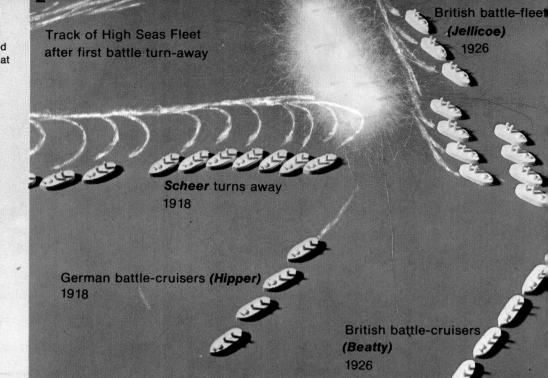

Track of High Seas Fleet after first battle turn-away

British battle-fleet *(Jellicoe)* 1926

Scheer turns away 1918

German battle-cruisers *(Hipper)* 1918

British battle-cruisers *(Beatty)* 1926

△ **Admiral Sir David Beatty.** During his running battle with Hipper's battle-cruisers, he sighted Scheer's fleet and set a course which led it into a trap.

The Eastern Front

Eastern Front 1914

RUSSIAN FORCES
GERMAN AND AUSTRIAN FORCES

100 MILES
150 KILOMETRES

Kovno

Gumbinnen

Danzig • **EAST PRUSSIA**

GERMANY

Masurian Lakes

Vistula R. Tannenberg

RUSSIA

• Warsaw

• Łódź

SILESIA • Lublin

RUSSIAN POLAND

Breslau

Kraków

AUSTRIA-HUNGARY Przemyśl • Lemberg

GALICIA

△ **Eastern Front August-December 1914.**
By the end of the year, the front was a line running 750 miles from Memel on the Baltic Sea to the northern borders of Bulgaria (not in the war until October 5, 1915). This long line covered different kinds of terrain, so it never became static like the Western Front.

Within ten days of entering World War One, Russia had two massive armies on the move against the Central Powers in the East. Although the Russian supply lines were far from properly organized, one army invaded East Prussia, the other Galicia.

These moves forced the Germans to withdraw some of their strength from the Western Front. In the fighting that followed, the Russians scored some early successes.

Then Hindenburg and Ludendorff took over command of the German forces and they crushed the Russians in battles at Tannenberg and Masurian Lakes. In Galicia, the Russians beat Austro-Hungarian forces in the Battle of Lemberg.

Meanwhile, the Serbs drove back three attempts at invasion by the Austrians. In 1915, Field-Marshal August von Mackensen, in command of combined German-Austrian armies, drove the Russians from Galicia, Poland and Lithuania and by the end of the year Serbia had been conquered.

Brusilov's brilliant offensive in 1916 turned the tide for the Russians for a time but, by the end of the year, the Eastern Front, stretching from the Baltic to the Sea of Azov, had been pushed 700 miles to the east.

For Russia, the war formally ended with the signing of the Treaty of Brest-Litovsk on March 3, 1918. By this treaty Finland, Estonia, Latvia, Poland, Lithuania, Bessarabia and the Ukraine, formerly part of Imperial Russia, became nations on their own (*cf* p. 51). The Tsar had been deposed and the treaty was signed for the Communists by Leon Trotsky.

△ **General Paul von Hindenburg (68) and the young (48) General Erich von Ludendorff** were in command of the German armies that crushed the Russians at Tannenberg and Masurian Lakes.

▷ **Austro-Hungarian troops looking after a wounded comrade.** The Austro-Hungarians suffered appalling casualties against the Russians. In the Battle of Lemberg, in 1914, they lost 250,000 men killed and wounded. In the Brusilov Offensive of 1916 they lost 200,000 killed. Their own efforts to dispose of Serbia failed until the Germans came to their assistance. In July 1916, Germany took command of almost the whole Eastern Front.

△ **Some of the thousands of Russian prisoners taken on the Eastern Front.** In winter, war came to a standstill in the intense cold. Snow, ice and blizzards made survival a problem in itself. On one night in winter, a German force lost 1,000 horses, all frozen to death. Cavalry was still a feature of fighting in the East.

The line stretched over many different kinds of terrain—plains, marshes, forests and mountains—and the fighting encompassed a vast area in parts of which people still tended their farms and worked peacefully.

In 1915, German strategy accepted a defensive role on the Western Front in order to destroy the Russian "steamroller" in the East. Despite poor equipment, the Russians put up a terrific resistance.

△ **A common sight on the Eastern Front: standard Russian Maxim gun.** Besides its wheeled mounting, it also had a gun shield (not shown) peculiar to the Russian-produced gun. It fired 7.62 mm. ammunition and could be raised on a tripod. The Russians manufactured small arms and machine-guns, but they had to obtain their field artillery from other countries. Infantry men used the M 1891 Moisin-Nagent 7.62 mm. rifle. Cavalry used either M 1891 dragoon rifle or M 1910 Moisin-Nagent, both 7.62 mm.

△ **Russian troops on the Galician front during the Brusilov Offensive.** Brusilov was ordered to attack in order to relieve pressure on the Allies in Trentino (Italy) and at Verdun on the Western Front. He achieved this aim. Austrian troops were rushed back from Italy and 35 German divisions were transferred from the Western Front. The attack began on June 4, 1916 and ended about August 10. But Brusilov received small help from his fellow generals. He said he could have won the war for the Allies. Experts agree that his Offensive saved the Allies from losing it.

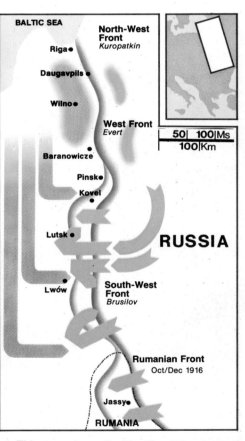

△ **This map shows the Brusilov Offensive.** The main thrust towards Lutsk and Kovel drove the Austrians back. At this stage, Brusilov was waiting for news that General Evert had attacked on the West Front in order to hold the German troops there. Instead, some of Evert's men were sent south to help Brusilov. At once, the Germans transferred troops from the West Front to face Brusilov, and his advance ground to a halt. Brilliant victory became crushing defeat.

31

The War in Arabia and Africa

David Lloyd George, Prime Minister of Britain, was talking in London in July 1917, to a large, handsome man, immaculately dressed in the uniform of a general in the British army. As they shook hands, the Prime Minister said, with a twinkle in his eye,

"Jerusalem by Christmas!" The big man was Sir Edmund Allenby, new commander of the British Army in Egypt.

In the Middle East, the war had been concerned with protecting the Suez Canal from the Turks, who occupied Palestine. But now Allenby was going to break out of the Allied line east of the Sinai Desert. Here the Turks had defied the Allies for months. Allenby shifted GHQ from the comfort of Cairo to Umm el Kalab (Mother of Dogs) in the desert and laid his plans.

The obvious point for an attack was at Gaza on the coast where a sea bombardment was possible. Allenby used a variety of tricks to make the Turks think he was going to attack Gaza. Then, on October 31, he attacked Beersheba at the other end of the line. Within a week, he had driven the Turks back from the Gaza-Beersheba line, and by December 9 he had advanced 50 miles, and taken Jerusalem.

He did not move on until September, 1918. Then once more he swept through the Turkish defences and in three days completed the conquest of Palestine. He drove on 200 miles to Aleppo in Syria where Turkey's military power was finally destroyed. Allenby's army had advanced 350 miles, taken 75,000 prisoners and captured 360 guns for the loss of only 5,000 men. On October 31, Turkey became the second of the Central Powers to ask for peace.

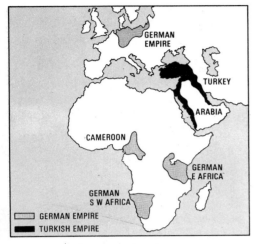

△ **This map shows the territories** which formed the German and Turkish Empires in Africa and Arabia in 1914.

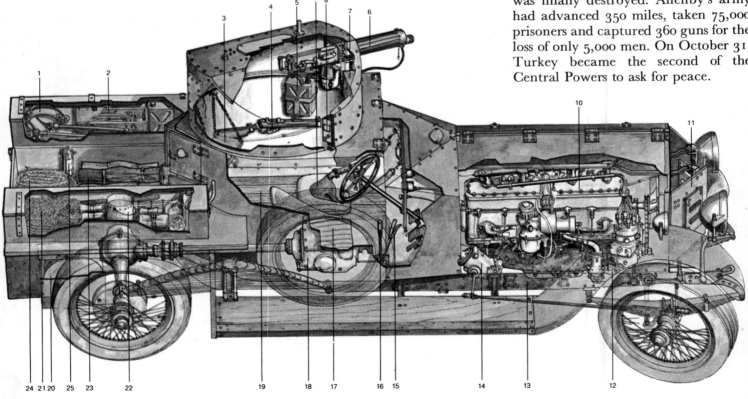

△ **Rolls-Royce Armoured Car.** Its speed and mobility combined with its firepower made it an invaluable asset in the desert war. Weight: 3.5 tons. Length: 16 ft. 7 in. Height: 7 ft. 6 in. Speed: 50 m.p.h. Armour: 8 mm. maximum. Mobility was a feature of Allenby's campaigns. He made a careful study of the terrain and routes in Palestine, referring every day to *Historical Geography of the Holy Land* by

George Adam Smith and to the Bible.
1 Tripod for machine gun (stored). **2** Tools.
3 Swing seat for optional fourth crew member. **4** Lee Enfield .303-inch rifle (one of three). **5** Can of water for machine-gun cooling. **6** Vickers .303-inch machine-gun.
7 Ammunition feed box. **8** Ammunition boxes slung round turret rim. **9** Straps for passenger back rest. **10** Rolls-Royce engine.

11 Armoured radiator doors (controlled from inside car). **12** Magneto. **13** Rolls-Royce Silver Ghost chassis. **14** Steering box.
15 Handbrake. **16** Gear lever. **17** Driver's seat. **18** Gear box. **19** Wooden floor. **20** Armoured petrol tank. **21** Locker for chains, ropes, personal items etc. **22** Cooker. **23** Blankets.
24 Tow ropes. **25** Fire extinguisher.

Lawrence of Arabia

In 1916, Arabs in the Middle East were in revolt against their Turkish overlords and a small group of British officers was sent to help them. One was Colonel T. E. Lawrence, who became famous as "Lawrence of Arabia."

He spoke Arabic and knew a great deal about Arab history and customs. He lived as an Arab, wearing Arab dress and eating Arab food. He helped the Arabs, led by the Emir Feisal, to attack Turkish outposts and towns and the railway running south of Medina. This was an important line of communication for the Turks.

Soon the Turks were offering rewards of £20,000 (alive) and £10,000 (dead) for "El Lorens." He was captured and tortured but the Turks did not realize who he was and he escaped.

After the war, Lawrence refused all honours and decorations, and lived under a false name. He told the story of his adventures in a famous book, *The Seven Pillars of Wisdom*. He died in a motorcycle accident in 1935.

△ **General Sir Edmund Allenby**, conqueror of Palestine. He lived in the field with his men and they nicknamed him "The Bull."

▽ **Colonel T. E. Lawrence** as "Lawrence of Arabia"—one of the most romantic figures of World War One, fated to be the subject of books, plays, film.

△ **Symbol of German defiance in Africa:** askari bearing the German Imperial flag.

The War in Africa

Germany's colonies in Africa were taken out of the war one by one. German South-West Africa gave in on July 9, 1915, after a short campaign by an army under General Louis Botha, Prime Minister of South Africa. The garrison in the Cameroons held out against British, French and Belgian troops until October 1915. They fled into Spanish Guinea and their commander and 6,000 men were interned. In German East Africa General Paul von Lettow-Vorbeck defied the Allies with a force of 5,000 men including only 50 from Europe. He only gave in when Germany herself asked for peace.

The Russian Revolution

Russia had long been seething with discontent but, for three years the Russian people fought stubbornly against the Germans, enduring enormous casualties, hunger and mismanagement at home and at the front. By 1917, they were on the verge of collapse.

In March, 1917 (February according to the Russian calendar), the people of Petrograd rioted for food. Soldiers joined in and the riot became a revolution. The Tsar, Nicholas II, abdicated and a Socialist government led by Alexander Kerensky tried to introduce democratic reforms and keep the war going. Meanwhile, Vladimir Lenin, leader of the extreme Bolshevik party, returned from exile to organize workers' soviets (councils) and to advocate peace with Germany. However, he was forced to flee to Finland.

When a Russian offensive failed and the half-starved soldiers deserted in thousands, Lenin's chance had come.

He and Leon Trotsky overthrew the Kerensky government and accepted Germany's harsh peace terms. By the Treaty of Brest-Litovsk, Russia gave up huge expanses of her territory but Lenin was prepared to pay the price for complete power. The Bolsheviks could now set to work to establish a Communist dictatorship and Russia was subjected to renewed sufferings as civil war raged for the next three years.

To the Allies, the Revolution was a disaster. It meant that Germany was free to transfer a million men to the Western Front and there was also the danger of revolutionary doctrines infecting the war-weary troops.

△ **Nicholas II, Tsar of Russia,** with his son and daughters and officers of the Imperial Guard. This photo reached Paris in March 1917, the month of the Tsar's abdication. The Communists killed the Tsar and his family in July 1918.

△ **Alexander Kerensky,** Prime Minister of the Russian Government in summer, 1917, seen touring the front to raise the morale of the troops. He left Petrograd when Lenin's followers were seizing power in the "October Revolution." He went to find loyal troops to suppress the uprising, but never came back. After he had gone, the leaderless government in the Winter Palace was beseiged, and, in the early hours of the next day, its members were arrested.

△ **Revolution scene in Petrograd:** crowds scatter as machine-guns begin to fire. The seeds of the "October Revolution" were sown in a revolution in 1905 in which, on "Bloody Sunday" January 22, the Tsar's guards opened fire on a procession and killed 1,500 people.

Тов. Ленин ОЧИЩАЕТ землю от нечисти.

△ **A Russian cartoon:** Lenin's was the "new brush that sweeps clean," by doing away with kings, capitalists and priests.

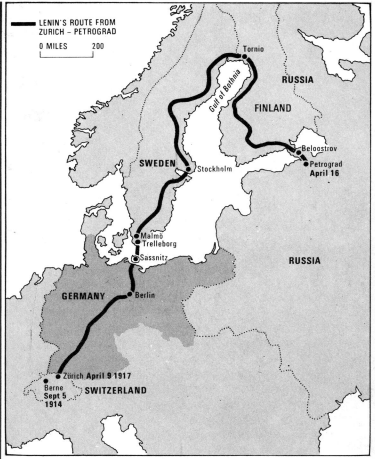

△ **Lenin's route to Russia, April 1917.** The moment Lenin read of the Tsar's downfall in a newspaper in Zürich in March, 1917, he decided to return to Russia. Only one route seemed possible, and that was through Germany. The Germans were ready to help, but he did not want to appear to be plotting with Russia's enemy. In the end, he travelled in a sealed compartment of a train and so had no contact with Germans on the journey.

▽ **Storming the Winter Palace** in Petrograd in November 1917 (October by the Russian calendar—hence "the October Revolution"). Romantic version of what happened by a Soviet artist. On the far left is the cruiser, *Aurora*, whose sailors reinforced the Bolshevik's Red Guards during the siege of the government. The Revolution was almost bloodless; only six people died in the attack on the Winter Palace.

Submarines at War

"It is impossible to go on with the war if losses like this continue",

said Admiral Jellicoe, First Sea Lord of the British Admiralty in 1917. He was referring to losses caused by German U-boats which, at this time, had reached a peak. In April 1917 over one million tons of shipping were sunk and one ship in every four leaving a British port was lost. With 105 U-boats in service, Germany had announced unrestricted submarine warfare. Enemy and neutral ships at sea would be torpedoed without warning.

△ Painting by Claus Bergen of major threat to the Allies—**a U-boat**.

△ **U9.** Length: 188 ft. Beam: 19¾ ft. Power: 1,050 h.p. diesel engines for travel on surface, or 1,160 h.p. electric engines for underwater. Speed: 14 knots on surface or 8 knots underwater. Armament: four 17.7-inch torpedo tubes, one 2-inch gun. Crew: 28. Germany began submarine warfare on February 4, 1915, declaring the waters around Britain a war zone. At this date, Germany only had 21 submarines. Yet they posed a problem for Allied shipping. The sea was Britain's lifeline and the U-boats aimed to cut it. In 1916, U-boats were sinking 400,000 tons of Allied shipping each month.

△ **In an attempt to clear the sea of mines** laid by the enemy, both sides used minesweepers. These ships were always at hazard by the nature of their work. This one has struck a mine and is sinking.

▽ **This map shows in white the areas where German U-boats were in action** after February 1, 1917. The immediate results were shocking for the Allies. But the convoy system and the use of mines defeated the submarine menace in time. First the English Channel was effectually blocked with mines forcing the U-boats to go north of Scotland to reach the shipping lanes in the Atlantic. From July 1917 a massive line of mines known as the Northern Barrage was being laid between the Orkney Islands and Norway. The task continued to the end of the war, 69,000 mines being laid in all.

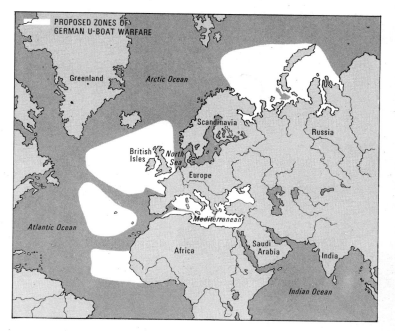

PROPOSED ZONES OF GERMAN U-BOAT WARFARE

Greenland

Arctic Ocean

Scandinavia

Russia

British Isles

North Sea

Europe

Atlantic Ocean

Mediterranean

Africa

Saudi Arabia

India

Indian Ocean

▽ **UB II.** Length 118½ ft. Beam: 14½ ft. Power: 284 h.p. Speed: 9 or 5¾ knots. Displacement: 263/292 tons. Armament: two 19.7-inch torpedo tubes, one 2-inch gun. Crew: 23. The Allies took two steps to ward off the stranglehold of the U-boats. Ships sailed in convoys, protected by warships; vast numbers of mines were laid in the seas around Britain, particularly in the English Channel. 17 U-boats were sunk by mines in 1917. Warships on U-boat patrol sank 16, warships with convoys sank six, and Q ships (warships disguised as merchant ships) sank six. In 1918, 69 more were sunk. The U-boat had lost.

Isolationist America

TAKE UP THE SWORD OF JUSTICE

△ **British poster** reminding people in the U.S. of the sinking of the *Lusitania* by a U-boat with the loss of 128 American lives.

When World War One began, the United States remained out of it. The President, Woodrow Wilson, remarked to the German Ambassador, "We have to be neutral. Otherwise, our mixed populations would wage war on each other."

Many Americans had relatives in countries on both sides in Europe. There were Americans of German descent, and some of Irish stock who had little love for the English.

Being neutral meant trying to be fair in dealing with countries on both sides of the war. Bankers in the United States were allowed to lend money to governments of the Allies and of the Central Powers.

Deciding what to do about providing supplies to the Allies was not so easy. Since Britain controlled the seas, her ships were able to sail to ports in the United States. Should these ships be allowed to pick up cargoes of raw materials and weapons? President Wilson decided that the United States had no right to deny the Allies what they wanted. The Germans would have received the same treatment. However, their ships were unable to reach America.

▽ **A group of American women** setting out to attend a peace conference in Holland, 1915. The flag was presented to them by the Mayor of New York and they were given a tumultuous send-off by their fellow-countrymen who, at this stage, still wanted neutrality.

PEACE

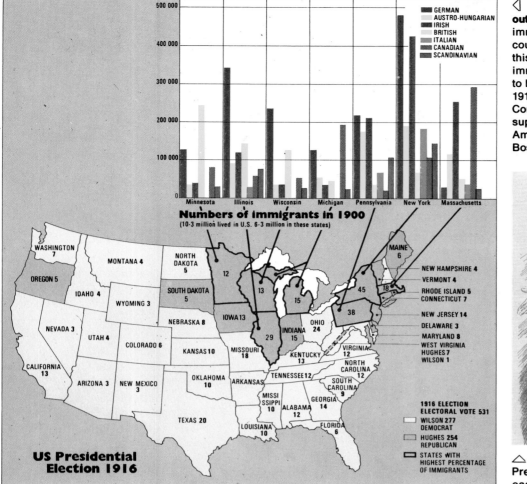

Numbers of immigrants in 1900
(10·3 million lived in U.S. 6·3 million in these states)

Chart legend:
- GERMAN
- AUSTRO-HUNGARIAN
- IRISH
- BRITISH
- ITALIAN
- CANADIAN
- SCANDINAVIAN

States on chart: Minnesota, Illinois, Wisconsin, Michigan, Pennsylvania, New York, Massachusetts

US Presidential Election 1916

State electoral votes shown on map:
WASHINGTON 7, OREGON 5, MONTANA 4, IDAHO 4, WYOMING 3, NORTH DAKOTA 5, SOUTH DAKOTA 5, NEBRASKA 8, NEVADA 3, UTAH 4, COLORADO 6, KANSAS 10, CALIFORNIA 13, ARIZONA 3, NEW MEXICO 3, OKLAHOMA 10, TEXAS 20, MINNESOTA 12, IOWA 13, MISSOURI 18, ARKANSAS, LOUISIANA 10, WISCONSIN 13, ILLINOIS 29, INDIANA 15, MICHIGAN 15, OHIO 24, KENTUCKY 13, TENNESSEE 12, MISSISSIPPI 10, ALABAMA 12, GEORGIA 14, FLORIDA 6, SOUTH CAROLINA 9, NORTH CAROLINA 12, VIRGINIA 12, WEST VIRGINIA HUGHES 7 WILSON 1, PENNSYLVANIA 38, NEW YORK 45, MARYLAND 8, DELAWARE 3, NEW JERSEY 14, MAINE 6, NEW HAMPSHIRE 4, VERMONT 4, RHODE ISLAND 5, CONNECTICUT 7

1916 ELECTION ELECTORAL VOTE 531
- WILSON 277 DEMOCRAT
- HUGHES 254 REPUBLICAN
- STATES WITH HIGHEST PERCENTAGE OF IMMIGRANTS

◁ **The population of the United States at the outbreak of war** included a great many immigrants, many of them with links with countries on both sides in the war. Note in this chart the numbers of German and Irish immigrants in particular. Both groups tended to be opposed to England and the Allies. In 1914, a German-American Literary Defence Committee distributed 60,000 pamphlets supporting the cause of Germany. An Irish-American newspaper attacked the Mayor of Boston for supporting Britain.

△ **Cartoon published in the magazine *Punch*.** President Wilson is saying to the American eagle, "Gee! What a dove I've made of you."

△ **Procession in celebration of Woodrow Wilson's** election as President of the United States in March 1913. Wilson studied law, history and political science, and became President of Princeton University. In 1910, he was elected Governor of the state of New Jersey, and this made him a national figure.

Although he believed that the United States must remain neutral, President Wilson had sympathy for the Allies. He thought of Britain as a democracy like the United States, whereas to him Germany was a militaristic society, and, if the Central Powers won the war, it seemed as if the United States might

be threatened. In 1914 Wilson believed the war would end in stalemate or in victory for the Allies. In 1916, he was re-elected as President of the United States on a peace programme. (See how the individual states voted in the chart above.)

America joins the War

The United States of America entered World War One on the side of the Allies on April 6, 1917. Four days earlier, President Wilson had told Congress that recent actions of the German government were "nothing less than war against the United States."

He was referring mainly to the introduction by Germany in February of unrestricted U-boat warfare, with its direct threat to American ships. Wilson had waited to see if, in fact, they carried out this threat, and in March four American ships had been sunk.

That same month the "Zimmerman Telegram" came to light (*cf* below). But the entry of the United States did not transform the war situation overnight. The richest nation in the world had a strong navy but only a small army.

△ **Scene: United States Congress.** Date: April 2, 1917. President Woodrow Wilson, after two and a half years of neutrality, is speaking in grave tones. He is advising Congress to declare war on Germany. The result is instantaneous. Everyone in the assembly leaps to his feet cheering, "America wants war." Wilson goes on, still grave, "The world must be made safe for democracy. To such a task we can dedicate our lives and our fortunes, everything."

△ **Dr Arthur Zimmerman,** the German Foreign Minister in 1917. A telegram from him to his embassy in Mexico City offered an alliance with Mexico and advised Mexico to attack the United States. A British agent obtained a copy of the "Zimmerman Telegram" and it was published in newspapers in the United States on March 1. The result: a demand for war against Germany.

▽ **Crowd waving flags on Broadway,** having heard that America has entered the war. Americans looked upon the war as a crusade in which they were fighting to protect democracy from the German military powers. Their entry into the war was greeted with enthusiasm by the nation and a number of rousing popular songs were written to mark the event.

△ **Medal awarded to mothers in the United States** whose sons were serving in the armed forces.

◁ **"Doughboy"—U.S. infantryman of 1917.** He wore a high-quality uniform of olive green, often with double seams. The campaign hat with a "Montana" peak was replaced by a steel helmet for trench warfare. The webbing belt has cartridge pouches attached and a smaller pouch containing field dressings. The doughboy carried a large canvas pack and his greatcoat and blanket roll fitted on top of it. The rifle shown was standard issue to U.S. infantrymen. It is the Springfield M1913, .30 calibre.

△ **Recruits to the United States Army on parade.** American troops turned the tide for the Allies, whose manpower had been "bled white" by the awful slaughter on the Western Front. But when the United States entered the war, she had only a quarter of a million men—a smaller army than Bulgaria had when she went to war. Millions of civilians had to be recruited and trained before they were ready to be sent to France. The first Americans reached France in June 1917 commanded by General John J. Pershing.

△ **Troops of the American Expeditionary Force** training in France. The 1st Division landed in France at the end of June 1917. But the 2nd Division did not follow until September. Not only had the United States to recruit her armies; she also had to ship them 3,000 miles.

Spies and Intelligence

In any war, an intelligence service can provide vital assistance for military commanders. Today, international espionage has been raised to a high art, employing a wide range of scientific devices (including artificial satellites).

But in 1914, intelligence was run on simpler lines. Most spies were ordinary persons carrying out uncomplicated tasks. It is said that the news that Russia had called up her armies was passed to Germany by a horse-and-cart trader from East Prussia. He took a notice from the wall of a post office over the border! The military commanders knew what information they wanted. Before the war, Russia and Germany collected information about each other's railways. (It took 4,000 train movements to prepare Germany's attack on Belgium.) In Britain, German spies observed dockyards and naval bases unaware that security agents were watching them. British spies watched Germany's docks and naval bases perhaps similarly observed.

▽ **A coded message** picked out on the teeth of a comb.

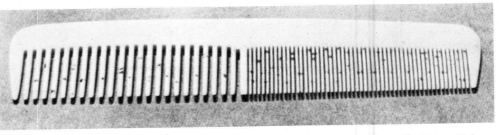

△ **A Belgian is searched by a German soldier** in case he is conveying information to the enemy. In a battle area, locals could obtain much information—names of regiments, number in a garrison, use of new equipment, etc.

▽ **A glass eye designed to contain messages.** Suspicion might fall on a spy at any time and it was important that he should not be found to possess anything to indicate his espionage activities. Spies devised many ingenious hiding places.

▽ **Passing on information called for a high degree of invention.** Codes allowed messages to pass undetected through enemy hands. This stamp was on an envelope containing a code message. Perforations on the stamp gave the key to the code.

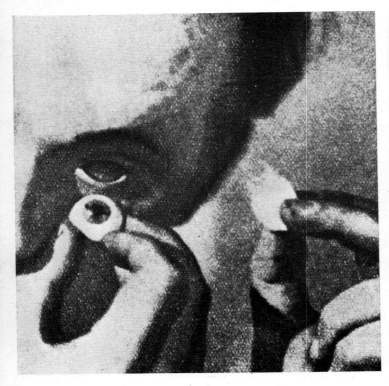

▽ **Field telephone and equipment** of kind used during the early fighting in the west. With messages passed by phone, there was risk of line-tapping. Wise spies used codes of innocent phrases.

△ **When soldiers disguised themselves in civilian clothes,** they ran the risk of being classed as spies and suffering the death penalty if caught. That risk was taken by these Frenchmen. They are escaped prisoners-of-war. The most famous spy of World War One was Margaretha Gertrude Zelle, a Dutch dancer, better known as Mata Hari. In 1914 she acted as a German agent in neutral Holland. Then in 1915 she went to

Paris and from there travelled nearer to the battlefront, performing her dances and mingling with the French officers. Later she offered to work for the French Secret Service. They soon knew she was a German spy but at first she was useful to them. In 1916, she went to Spain and on her return she was arrested. After a trial she was found guilty of spying and shot. She left behind a legend of a beautiful master-spy.

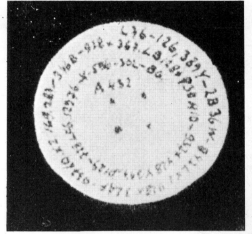

△ **Another hiding place.** A button is split in two. Printed on it, inside, is a coded message.

▽ **The code messages in this picture** are in the shading in the cross and the circle. Secret messages were encoded in a wide variety of ways, not all of them using letters or figures. Codes were broken down by experts called cryptanalysts.

▽ **On the face of it, a sheet of music.** Actually, a secret message. Cryptanalysts or code-breakers were patient and persistent. They knew that, in time, they could crack any code. Their problem: to decode *while the message was still valuable.*

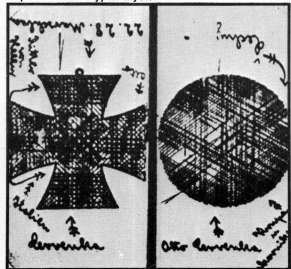

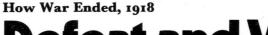

Defeat and Victory

"With our backs to the wall and believing in the justice of our cause, each one of us must fight to the end." This order of the day was issued on April 12, 1918 by the British commander, Field-Marshal Haig. There had been a new German offensive.

It had opened a gap 30 miles wide in the Allied line in Flanders. Already the Germans had driven the Allies back 40 miles at St Quentin and in May they began a drive for Paris. By July, the second Battle of the Marne had begun. But this was Germany's final throw. In August, the Allies counter-attacked and the Germans crumbled. One month later Marshal Foch, in charge of all Allied armies, ordered a general advance and this did not stop until the Germans asked for peace on November 7. World War One was effectually over.

△ **Marshal Henri Philippe Omer Pétain** (1856-1951)—symbol of what the Battle of Verdun did to France. Holding the fortress cost 315,000 men and the heart of the French Army. After the war, Pétain supported the ill-fated Maginot Line as a defence for France. When France was overrun in World War Two, he made terms with the Germans. With peace, he was tried for treason and condemned to death but imprisoned instead.

△ **The Belgian town of Ypres,** houses wrecked, streets destroyed, with here and there huge, water-filled craters. Ypres was the scene of three bloody battles. These were the homes to which people would be returning with peace; this was the desolation they had to contend with.

△ **C 19 tank** of the Heavy Section British Machine Gun Corps. In the final stages of the war, the Allies made good use of the tank—a weapon the Germans were slow to exploit. In August 1918 when the British and French made a combined attack on the Somme, 450 tanks were used.

▷ **Desolation after battle on the Western Front.** Mud was one of the horrors of war. It meant not only discomfort but also danger. General Sir Hubert Gough wrote, "Men of the strongest physique could hardly move forward at all and became easy victims to the enemy's snipers."

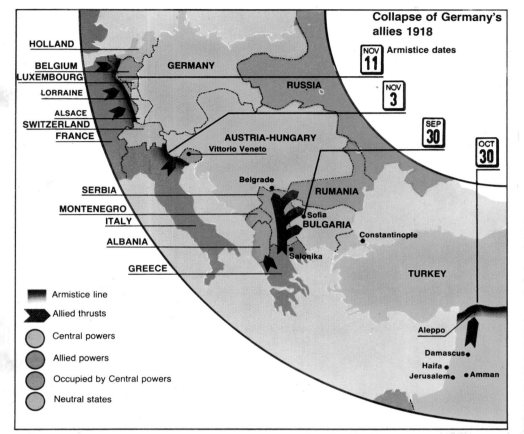

Collapse of Germany's allies 1918

NOV 11 Armistice dates

NOV 3

SEP 30

OCT 30

HOLLAND
BELGIUM
LUXEMBOURG
LORRAINE
ALSACE
SWITZERLAND
FRANCE
GERMANY
RUSSIA
AUSTRIA-HUNGARY
Vittorio Veneto
Belgrade
SERBIA
MONTENEGRO
ITALY
ALBANIA
GREECE
RUMANIA
Sofia
BULGARIA
Salonika
Constantinople
TURKEY
Aleppo
Damascus
Haifa
Jerusalem • Amman

Armistice line
Allied thrusts
Central powers
Allied powers
Occupied by Central powers
Neutral states

△ **This map summarises the end of the World War One.** Serbian, French and Senegalese infantry on September 15, launched the attack which was to take Bulgaria out of the war. It was supported by another attack by British and Greeks and soon aircraft of the Royal Air Force were wiping out enemy columns on roads inside Bulgaria. Riots broke out in four towns, and the Bulgars asked for peace. Similar offensives took out Turkey and Austria-Hungary.

△ **Marshal Foch** (second right) in front of the coach where he accepted the German surrender.

△ **Canadian soldier** resting with captured German during the German 1918 spring offensive.

The Peace Terms

Marshal Ferdinand Foch, General in Chief of the Allied Armies in the West, received a small group of Germans at his headquarters in the Forest of Compiègne on November 7, 1918. They wanted peace. Foch told them the Allied terms: Germans to leave all occupied territory, to surrender their arms and warships, withdraw all forces from west of the River Rhine, return Allied prisoners, allow Allied troops to occupy German territory.

Foch gave the Germans 72 hours to decide their answer and he had it by November 9. On November 11, at 5 am German delegates entered a railway coach in the Forest of Compiègne to sign the armistice. Fighting stopped on all battlefronts at 11 am.

△ **Wounded German** carried on a stretcher by South African Scots.

The Cost of the War

How do you measure the cost of a war? In casualties perhaps. In this respect, World War One was the bloodiest war in history up to its time. More than 8 million men died in combat and 20 million were wounded. Germany lost 2 million men.

France lost 1,358,000—a graver loss with her smaller population. Great Britain lost three-quarters of a million men and the Empire a quarter of a million more.

Russia lost one and three-quarter millions and was to lose more in civil war. The United States lost relatively few—114,095. The total number of civilian casualties was about 22 million.

Where the fighting occurred, land was laid waste. In France alone, 1,875 square miles of forest was destroyed and 8,000 square miles of farming land torn up. Yet on the map of Europe, the areas of destruction seem small and they were largely restored within a few years of the war's end.

But in the complex area of international finance the war left a more lasting scar. Before the war's start, people had been saying that there would never again be a large-scale war.

The men who handle money matters at the international level are the guardians of world prosperity. It was said that they were so powerful that they could prevent war by pointing out what it would cost in terms of money.

But the financiers failed in 1914. And after World War One, faith in them was shattered. In the next two decades, the world was plagued with economic problems.

△ **A grim reminder of the carnage of war.** Postwar photograph of rows of graves in the military cemetery of Polygon Wood at Zonnebeke.

▽ **Rising prices:** with sea trade reduced by war and farming affected by damage to land or lack of men to work it, food became scarce in many countries.

△ **These women are queueing for rations in Prague.** Many countries were so short of food that they introduced systems of rationing, each person being permitted to buy limited amounts of some foods. Even so, the rations were often not supplied in full.

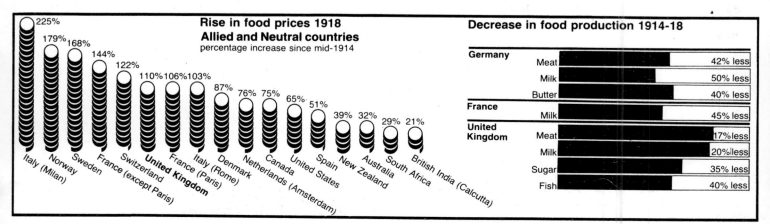

Rise in food prices 1918
Allied and Neutral countries
percentage increase since mid-1914

- 225% Italy (Milan)
- 179% Norway
- 168% Sweden
- 144% France (except Paris)
- 122% Switzerland
- 110% United Kingdom
- 106% France (Paris)
- 103% Italy (Rome)
- 87% Denmark
- 76% Netherlands (Amsterdam)
- 75% Canada
- 65% United States
- 51% Spain
- 39% New Zealand
- 32% Australia
- 29% South Africa
- 21% British India (Calcutta)

Decrease in food production 1914-18

Germany		
Meat		42% less
Milk		50% less
Butter		40% less
France		
Milk		45% less
United Kingdom		
Meat		17% less
Milk		20% less
Sugar		35% less
Fish		40% less

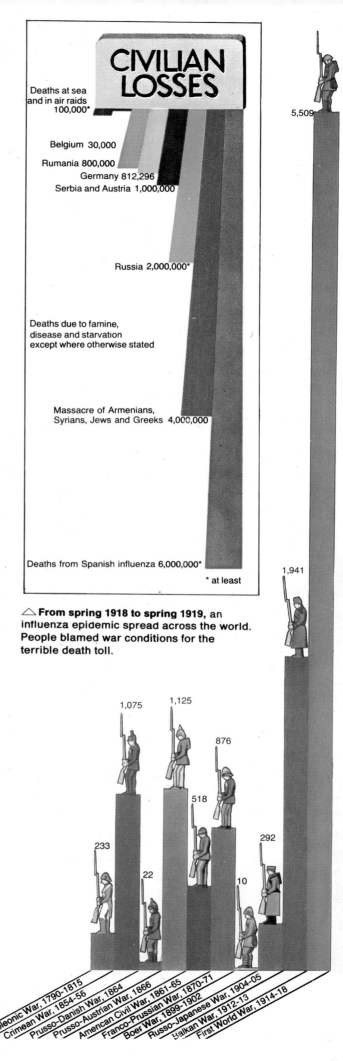

CIVILIAN LOSSES

Deaths at sea and in air raids 100,000*

Belgium 30,000

Rumania 800,000

Germany 812,296

Serbia and Austria 1,000,000

Russia 2,000,000*

Deaths due to famine, disease and starvation except where otherwise stated

Massacre of Armenians, Syrians, Jews and Greeks 4,000,000

Deaths from Spanish influenza 6,000,000*

* at least

△ **From spring 1918 to spring 1919,** an influenza epidemic spread across the world. People blamed war conditions for the terrible death toll.

△ **A French painting** of a parade of war-wounded in Paris, a week after armistice was signed.

▷ **Military loss of life per day during World War One,** compared with previous wars. The total number of deaths was accounted for as follows (approximate figures only):

Germany	2,000,000	Italy	460,000
Russia	1,700,000	Turkey	375,000*
France	1,358,000	British Empire	251,900
Austria-Hungary	1,100,000	United States	114,000
Great Britain	760,000	*At least	

The dead represented the cream of each nation's manhood, men in the very prime of life. Worst hit in this sense was France comparing her losses to her population. It was said that the Battle of Verdun left a scar on France that it took a generation to remove. Many historians believe that the Russian figure given here is an under-estimate. A.J.P.Taylor wrote, ''Russia probably lost more [men] than all the rest put together.''

5,509

1,941

1,075   1,125

876

518

233

22   10   292

Napoleonic War, 1790-1815
Crimean War, 1854-56
Prusso-Danish War, 1864
Prusso-Austrian War, 1866
American Civil War, 1861-65
Franco-Prussian War, 1870-71
Boer War, 1899-1902
Russo-Japanese War, 1904-05
Balkan War, 1912-13
First World War, 1914-18

The Blighted Peace

△ **This happy French soldier is back home,** re-united with his wife and child. The end of the war brought delirious happiness. People danced in the streets. A bonfire was lit in Trafalgar Square, London.

On January 18, 1919, the Peace Conference opened in Paris. It was to be a council of ten – two representatives from each of the great powers: Great Britain, France, Italy, Japan and the United States. But three men dominated the discussions –

President Woodrow Wilson of the United States, David Lloyd George, Prime Minister of Britain, and Georges Clemenceau, Premier of France. Wilson had produced 14 points as a basis for settlement. They included freedom of navigation, reduction in armaments, adjustments of colonial claims, independence for Poland, the people of Austria-Hungary to have opportunities for national development, and the setting up of an association of nations. He wanted the Allies to agree to "self-determination" for small nations. This meant that they could be independent if they wanted. But Britain and France did not accept this principle. Some of the Allies gained new possessions as a result of the war.

Finally five separate peace treaties were offered to the Central Powers. The Germans signed the Treaty of Versailles, by which the size of the country was reduced by one-eighth. She lost all her colonies (*cf* p. 51 for details). She was barred from having a navy and the size of her army was limited.

The job of seeing that the treaty was kept was given to the League of Nations which set up headquarters at Geneva in Switzerland. The League was supposed to solve international disputes in the future but it was not a success. The United States never joined the League of Nations.

△ **On June 28, 1919, the Treaty of Versailles was signed** in the Hall of Mirrors in the Palace of Versailles near Paris. This detail from the painting by Sir William Orpen shows the two Germans, Johannes Bell (seated) and Hermann Muller at the moment of signing. Watching are (seated) Henry White, Robert Lansing, Wilson, Clemenceau, Lloyd George, Bonar Law, Lord Balfour. When the victors had added their signatures, guns were fired. The first Germans sent to sign the treaty had resigned when they saw the terms.

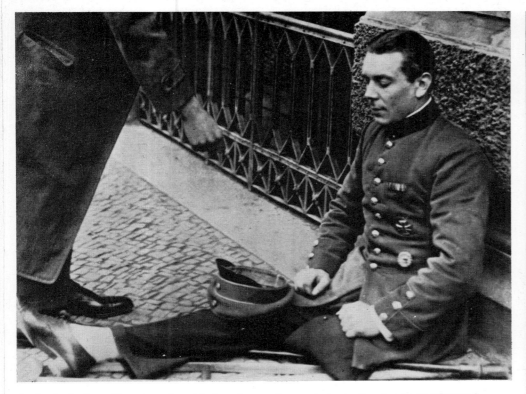

△ **A crippled ex-officer** is reduced to begging—grim reminder in the streets of shattered Germany. For victors and vanquished, the problems of the war did not vanish overnight.

PEACE AND FUTURE CANNON FODDER

The Tiger: "Curious! I seem to hear a child weeping!"

△ **The victors agreed** that Germany must make reparations for losses they had caused. German property in Allied countries was to be sold. In Berlin, these Germans protested.

◁ **In this incredibly prophetic cartoon,** the French Premier, Georges Clemenceau, nicknamed "The Tiger," is shown leaving the peace conference with Lloyd George, Vittorio Orlando of Italy and President Wilson, while somewhere a child weeps. A baby born in 1919 would have been 21 in 1940—ripe to provide "cannon fodder" for World War Two.

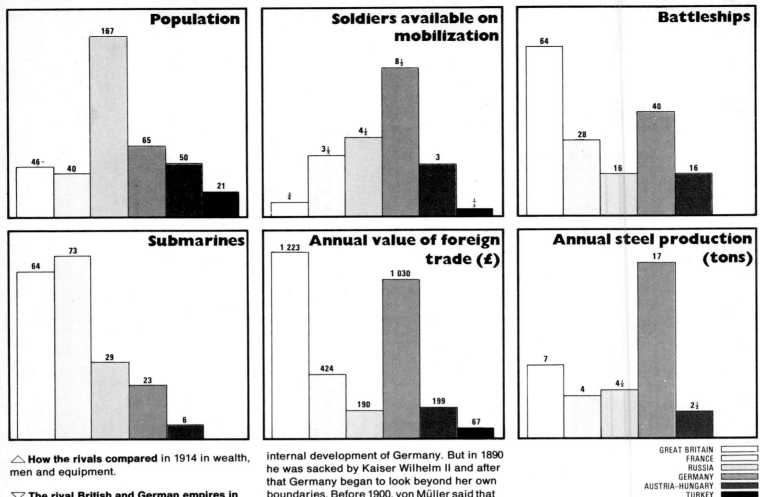

Population

167
65
50
46
40
21

Soldiers available on mobilization

8½
4½
3½
3
¾
⅓

Battleships

64
40
28
16
16

Submarines

73
64
29
23
6

Annual value of foreign trade (£)

1 223
1 030
424
190
199
67

Annual steel production (tons)

17
7
4
4½
2½

△ **How the rivals compared** in 1914 in wealth, men and equipment.

▽ **The rival British and German empires in 1914.** The German Empire emerged after the Franco-Prussian War of 1870-1. Bismarck, the German leader, was more concerned with the internal development of Germany. But in 1890 he was sacked by Kaiser Wilhelm II and after that Germany began to look beyond her own boundaries. Before 1900, von Müller said that Germany must aim at "the destruction of English world domination" to acquire colonies for the mid-European states.

GREAT BRITAIN
FRANCE
RUSSIA
GERMANY
AUSTRIA–HUNGARY
TURKEY
(ALL FIGURES IN MILLIONS
EXCEPT BATTLESHIPS
AND SUBMARINES)

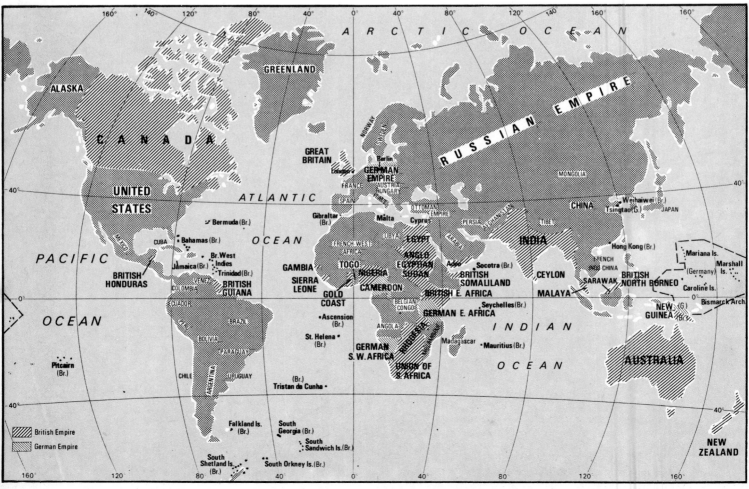

British Empire
German Empire

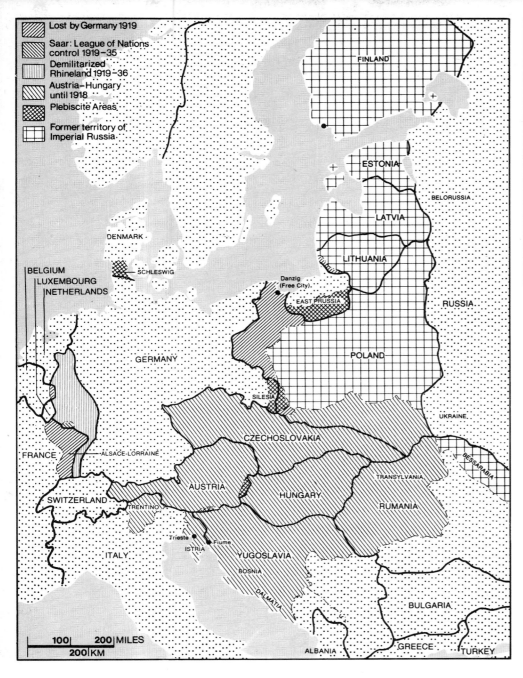

Lost by Germany 1919

Saar: League of Nations control 1919–35

Demilitarized Rhineland 1919–36

Austria–Hungary until 1918

Plebiscite Areas

Former territory of Imperial Russia

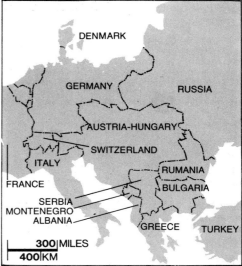

△ **The mainland of Europe before 1914.** Four great powers dominated the map—France, Germany, Austria-Hungary and Russia—with Italy in the south a near-great power. In Central Europe is the small group of Balkan states involved in wars in 1912 and '13—a group in which men of many races were still looking for a national identity such as Germany and Italy had found not long before. This was the trigger mechanism of World War One. Germany possessed the explosive.

◁ **Europe after the peace treaties.** From the Austro-Hungarian Empire came three new states—Austria, Hungary, and Czechoslovakia. The South Slavs, some of them formerly ruled by Austria-Hungary, have joined the old kingdom of Montenegro and Serbia to form a new nation, Yugoslavia. Italy and Rumania have gained large areas of Austro-Hungarian territory. Poland has been reformed from Russian, Austrian and German territory. Among other changes, France has regained Alsace-Lorraine (lost in the Franco-Prussian War) and Greece has gained Bulgarian territory on the Aegean Sea. Once more the map of Europe has been redrawn by history.

◁ **The cost of war for Imperial Germany.** This map shows how Germany's overseas possessions were disposed of, following the Treaty of Versailles. Woodrow Wilson, President of the United States, said that Germany's colonies should not simply be swallowed up by the victorious nations. Instead they should be known as mandated territories or mandates, being looked after by the conquerors on behalf of the League of Nations. All matters concerning them should be decided by reference to the League of Nations.

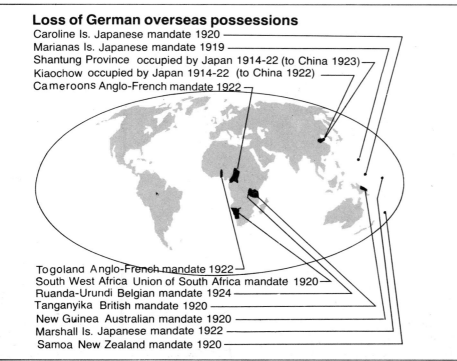

Loss of German overseas possessions

Caroline Is. Japanese mandate 1920
Marianas Is. Japanese mandate 1919
Shantung Province occupied by Japan 1914-22 (to China 1923)
Kiaochow occupied by Japan 1914-22 (to China 1922)
Cameroons Anglo-French mandate 1922

Togoland Anglo-French mandate 1922
South West Africa Union of South Africa mandate 1920
Ruanda-Urundi Belgian mandate 1924
Tanganyika British mandate 1920
New Guinea Australian mandate 1920
Marshall Is. Japanese mandate 1922
Samoa New Zealand mandate 1920

Why War Began...

The Main Events 1914-1918

What caused World War One? Many books have been written in an attempt to answer this question, and no doubt many more will be written, for there is no simple answer.

In 1914, the political map of Europe was dominated by five great powers—Austria-Hungary, Great Britain, France, Germany and Russia and one near-great power, Italy. Among these nations, there was an uneasy balance of power and they formed alliances for self-protection. Austria-Hungary, Germany and Italy formed the Triple Alliance. France, Russia and Britain formed the Triple Entente—a pact of friendship rather than an alliance. They were ready to help each other, but, in the case of Britain, not in unlimited terms.

German expansion
The seeds of World War One were sown in the 19th century. Some say that the seeds started to sprout early in the 20th century. Then Germany began to envy the colonies of Britain and France.

In 1905, she quarrelled with France over Morocco. Germany said that she would help Morocco resist France to keep her independence. In the event, France agreed to look after the financial affairs of Morocco and to organise her police force. Some say this was a victory for Germany; some say it was a victory for France. But one thing is certain. This incident drove France and Britain closer together.

In 1911, another crisis blew up over Morocco when the Germans sent a gunboat there, supposedly to "protect their interests." Again Britain said she was ready to help France in the event of war. But an agreement was reached.

The Balkan Wars
Meantime, in Eastern Europe, small nations were stirring restlessly against the might of Austria-Hungary and the declining Ottoman Empire, including Turkey, which was known as "the sick man of Europe." Some Hungarians saw Serbia as a threat to Austria-Hungary, and in 1912 and '13, two wars were fought. In the First Balkan War, Montenegro, Serbia, Greece and Rumania defeated Turkey. In the Second Balkan War, Serbia, Greece, Rumania and Turkey defeated Bulgaria.

Serbia emerged from these wars with half a million more people and as a military power of some strength, and the earlier fears of Austro-Hungarians were confirmed.

The chain-reaction begins
Serbia was implicated in the death of the Archduke Franz Ferdinand, heir to the throne of Austria-Hungary, at Sarajevo, and provided Austria-Hungary with an excuse to go to war with her. Russia was pledged to help Serbia and Germany had promised to help Austria-Hungary. World War One was then inevitable.

The opinion of the experts is divided, and the evidence is conflicting. Russia may not have intended to provoke Germany into action when she called up her armies. Perhaps she only intended to make Austria-Hungary back down. Threats of war were the every-day currency of diplomatic exchanges before World War One. But according to many experts, the calling up of armies was an irreversible step. Ministers of those days believed "mobilisation means war." Yet Russia was ill-fitted for a major war, and there is some evidence that Germany did not hurry to put her armies into the field. On the other hand, the German Chancellor, Bethmann-Hollweg, said that once the dice were set rolling, nothing could stop them. The assassination at Sarajevo set the dice rolling and nothing stopped them until 22 million people had died.

1914

△ **Sarajevo:** after the assassination, Princip is arrested.

28 June	Archduke Franz Ferdinand and wife assassinated.
5 July	Germany promises Austria-Hungary full support against Serbia.
23 July	Austria-Hungary makes demands on Serbia, to be settled within 48 hours.
24 July	Russia decides to defend Serbia in the event of attack by Austria-Hungary.
25 July	Austria-Hungary advises Russia: We do not intend to take any land from Serbia. Serbia's reply to ultimatum deemed to be unsatisfactory. Austria-Hungary calls up her armies.
26 July	Great Britain proposes an international conference to settle the dispute between Austria-Hungary and Serbia. Austria-Hungary and Germany reject the idea.
28 July	Austria-Hungary declares war on Serbia.
30 July	Russia calls up her armies.
31 July	Germany sends warning to Russia: Stop troop movements near German border within 24 hrs.
1 Aug	No reply received by Germany from Russia. Germany declares war on Russia.
3 Aug	Germany declares war on France. Italy announces: We will remain neutral.
4 Aug	Germany invades Belgium. Great Britain declares war on Germany.
6 Aug	Austria-Hungary declares war on Russia. Serbia declares war on Germany.
7 Aug	French troops enter Belgium.
8 Aug	Montenegro declares war on Germany.
12 Aug	Russians invade East Prussia.
14 Aug	French offensive in Lorraine.
16 Aug	British Expeditionary Force lands in France.
20 Aug	Germans enter Brussels.
21 Aug	BEF goes into action in Belgium.
23 Aug	British retreat from Mons begins. Japan declares war on Germany.
29 Aug	Germans defeat Russians at Tannenberg (East Prussia).
6-15 Sept	Germans beat Russians at Masurian Lakes.
Sept	Battle of Marne (France) begins.
14 Sept	German withdrawal ends at River Aisne (France).
29 Oct	Turkey enters war on side of Germany.
30 Oct	First Battle of Ypres (Belgium) begins.
5 Nov	Great Britain declares war on Turkey.
11 Nov	German offensive at Ypres. Trench warfare begins on Western Front.
14 Nov	Russians drive westward through Poland.
16 Nov	Germans counter-attack. Fighting to early December when Russians withdraw.

1915

14 Jan	Gen. Botha crosses Orange River from Union of South Africa and captures Swakopmund in German South-West Africa.
15 Jan	Britain decides on invasion of Gallipoli Peninsula (Turkey).
19-20 Jan	First Zeppelin attack on Britain. Bombs dropped at King's Lynn (Norfolk).
2 Feb	Turks try to cross Suez Canal near Ismailia.
4 Feb	German government declares waters around Britain a "war zone" and begins first unrestricted submarine campaign, which lasts until August.
1 Mar	Britain declares blockade of Germany.
18 Mar	Attempt by Allied fleet to sail through Dardanelles Strait (Turkey) fails.
22 Mar	Russians defeat Austrians, capture Przemysl (Poland).
22 Apr-25 May	Second Battle of Ypres. Germans use poison gas for the first time (23 Apr).
25 Apr	First Allied landings in Gallipoli at five places on tip of peninsula.
26 Apr	By Treaty of London, Italy joins war on side of Allies.
2 May	Austro-German offensive in Galicia. Germans win Battle of Gorlice-Tarnow.
7 May	Lusitania sunk by German U-boat off Queenstown, Ireland. 124 Americans among the dead.

△ Medals commemorating sinking of the *Lusitania*.

8 May	First phase of Gallipoli campaign ends. Allies have suffered heavy casualties, made little headway.
14 May	Germans capture Jaroslaw and advance into the Ukraine.
2 June	Italians cross Isonzo River, north-west of Trieste, and attack Austrians. Austrians withdraw.
3 June	Germans capture Przemysl (Poland).
9 July	Conquest of German South-West Africa is completed.
4 Aug	Germans capture Warsaw.
6 Aug	Further Allied landings in Gallipoli at Suvla Bay.
12 Aug	First enemy ship sunk by a torpedo launched from a British seaplane during Gallipoli operation.
20 Aug	Italy declares war on Turkey.
6 Sept	Bulgaria enters war on side of Central Powers. Germans capture Vilna, capital of Lithuania.
25-30 Sept	Renewed French attack at Souchez towards Vimy Ridge.
25 Sept -4 Oct	British attack at Loos, in support of French at Souchez.
28 Sept	Turks defeated at Kut-el-Amara.
6 Oct	Austro-German attack on Serbia. British and French troops now in Serbia to help Serbs.
9 Oct	Central Powers capture Belgrade (Serbia).
11 Oct	Bulgarians invade Serbia.
19-20 Dec	Some Allied troops evacuated from Gallipoli.

1916

8 Jan	Allied evacuation of Gallipoli Peninsula complete.
21 Feb	Battle of Verdun (France) begins.
27 Feb	Austrians capture Durazzo from Italians.
9 Mar	Portugal declares war on Germany.
11 Mar	Germany declares war on Portugal.
19 Mar–30 Apr	After Battle of Lake Naroch, Russians withdraw with heavy losses.
29 Apr	British and Indians surrender to Turks at Kut-el-Amara (Mesopotamia).
15 May–3 June	Austrians successful in attack on Italians in the Trentino.
31 May–1 June	Battle of Jutland. (German: Battle of Skagerrak).

△Casualty of **Battle of Jutland:** German battleship with hole torn by British shell.

4 June	Brusilov Offensive against Hungary starts.
1 July	Battle of Somme begins.
11 July	Verdun: last German assault.
14 Aug	Brusilov Offensive comes to an end.
17 Aug	Rumania signs alliance with Russia.
27 Aug	Italy declares war on Germany. Rumania declares war on Austria-Hungary.
28 Aug	Germany declares war on Rumania.
29 Aug	Hindenburg and Ludendorff, successful commanders on Eastern Front, in command of German forces on Western Front.
30 Aug	Turkey declares war on Rumania.
1 Sept	Bulgaria declares war on Rumania.
2-3 Sept	First German airship shot down over Britain.
15 Sept	Tanks used for first time in any war by British on Somme.
7 Nov	Woodrow Wilson re-elected President of the United States.
18 Nov	Battle of the Somme ends.
5 Dec	Bucharest (capital of Rumania) captured by Germans.
7 Dec	New Prime Minister of Britain, David Lloyd George.
12 Dec	Nivelle replaces Joffre as French Commander-in-Chief. German Chancellor issues peace note showing Germany ready to negotiate peace. Lloyd George rejects note (30 Dec).
18 Dec	Battle of Verdun ends.

1917

1 Feb	Germany announces unrestricted submarine warfare.
1 Mar	Zimmerman Telegram published in USA.
11 Mar	British troops enter Baghdad.
12 Mar	Revolution in Russia begins.
15 Mar	Nicholas II, Tsar of Russia, gives up throne.
27 Mar	Turks defeated by British at Gaza.
6 Apr	USA declares war on Germany.
7 Apr	Cuba declares war on Germany.
9 Apr	Successful British attack at Arras.
10 Apr	Canadians capture Vimy Ridge.
16 Apr–21 May	French attack in Second Battle of Aisne.
16 Apr	Lenin arrives in Russia.
10 May	First convoy sails from British port.
15 May	Pétain succeeds Nivelle as French C-in-C.
19 May	US government decides to send army to France.
20 May	First German submarine sunk by an aircraft.
25 May	First big daylight raid by German Gothas on Britain.
29 June	Gen. Allenby takes over Allied command on Palestine Front.
16 July	Russian retreat begins.
31 July	Third Battle of Ypres begins. (Last phase known as Battle of Passchendaele).
10 Sept	Kerensky becomes leader of Russia.
15 Sept	Provisional government declares Russia to be a republic.
4 Oct	British victory at Passchendaele Ridge.
24 Oct	Italians defeated at Caporetto by Austrians and Germans.
31 Oct	British attack Turkish line at Beersheba. In a week, the line is broken.
7 Nov	Third Battle of Ypres ends when British capture ruins of Passchendaele village.
8 Nov	Lenin announces soviet control of Russia. He is made leader.
16 Nov	New French Prime Minister: Clemenceau.
20 Nov	British victory at Cambrai using 381 tanks.
21 Nov	Russia asks Germany for peace.
5 Dec	Armistice between Germany and Russia.
7 Dec	USA declares war on Austria-Hungary.
9 Dec	Jerusalem captured by British.
22 Dec	Russia and Germany start peace negotiations.
31 Dec	Germans attack at Cambrai using flame-throwers.

△**Allied and German walking wounded** resting on way to dressing station.

1918

△**The grim toll of war:** dying and dead lie together after battle on the Western Front.

8 Jan	President Wilson announces a 14-point peace plan.
3 Mar	Russia signs peace treaty with Central Powers at Brest-Litovsk.
21 Mar	German offensive on Western Front begins with attack on Somme.
14 Apr	Gen. Foch is appointed C-in-C of all Allied armies on Western Front.
9 Apr	German offensive in Flanders begins.
23 Apr	Guatemala declares war on Germany.
7 May	Rumania signs peace treaty with Central Powers.
27 May	Germans break through Allied line on the Marne.
1 June	US troops drive back Germans at Château-Thierry.
14 June	German offensive on Western Front ends.
15 July	New German offensive on Western Front. This proves to be the last.
18 July	Allied counter-offensive on Western Front. First stage begins.
8 Aug	Second stage begins. Allies advance to River Rhine.
18 Aug	British advance in Flanders begins.
11 Sept	Allies break through Hindenburg Line.
26 Sept	New Allied offensive on Western Front. This proves to be the last.
30 Sept	Bulgarians sign armistice. British enter Sofia.
1 Oct	Ludendorff asks German government to negotiate for peace.
2 Oct	British capture Damascus.
3 Oct	French capture St Quentin.
4 Oct	Germans ask for armistice.
8 Oct	Hindenburg Line captured.
24 Oct	Italians defeat Austrians in Battle of Vittorio Veneto.
25 Oct	Scheer recalls U-boats.
29 Oct	German sailors mutiny.
30 Oct	Turkey signs armistice.
31 Oct	War in Middle East ends.
2 Nov	Hungary declares its independence.
3 Nov	Austria signs armistice.
7 Nov	Hungary signs armistice.
9 Nov	Kaiser Wilhelm II gives up throne of Germany. Germany becomes a republic.
11 Nov	Armistice with Germany signed by Allies. Fighting on Western Front ends at 11am.
29 Nov	King Nicholas of Montenegro deposed. Montenegro unites with Serbia.

Allenby, Edmund Henry Hynman, 1st Viscount (1861-1936). Served on the Western Front 1914-17, starting as a brilliant cavalry officer. In 1917, he became commander of the British Army in the Middle East and in October-December advanced from the Gaza-Beersheba line to Jerusalem. He conquered Palestine and went on to capture Damascus in October 1918, after which the Turks sought peace.

Balfour, Arthur James, 1st Earl of Balfour (1848-1930), British statesman. He was First Lord of the Admiralty from 1915, and as such was criticized for the way in which the outcome of the Battle of Jutland was made public. As Foreign Minister in 1916, he negotiated with the U.S. government about plans for the American entry into the war. It was he who stated in 1917 that Britain favoured the setting up of a national home for the Jews in Palestine after the war (the "Balfour Declaration").

Beatty, David, 1st Earl (1871-1936), British admiral. At the war's start sailed into Heligoland Bight and sank three German cruisers. In January 1915, he chased German battle cruisers in the North Sea and sank the *Blücher*. At the Battle of Jutland, his battle cruisers fought the hardest sea action of the war. He succeeded Lord Jellicoe (*cf* below) as Commander-in-Chief of the grand fleet in 1916 and became First Sea Lord in 1919. For his services at Jutland he was awarded £100,000 and an earldom.

Botha, Louis (1862-1919), South African general and statesman. First Premier of South Africa 1910-1919. He declared war on Germany in 1914, and agreed to the invasion of German Southwest Africa by the forces of the Union of South Africa. This provoked a revolt among the South Africans themselves, which he suppressed. In July 1915, German Southwest Africa was taken by his forces. He attended the peace talks at Versailles, but died on his return to South Africa and was succeeded by Smuts (*cf* below).

Brusilov, Alexei Alexeievich (1853-1926), Russian C.-in-C., June-August 1917. Brusilov's Offensive against the Austro-Hungarians in June-August 1916 was immensely successful, disposing of 600,000 enemy troops killed and captured. It is the only event of the war named after the military commander responsible for it.

Brusilov

Enver Pasha

Briand, Aristide (1862-1932), Prime Minister of France from 1915 to 1917. In all, he was eleven times Prime Minister, 16 times Foreign Minister, three times Minister of Justice, four times Minister of the Interior and twice Minister of Education. As Foreign Minister, he strongly supported the League of Nations. He was given the Nobel Peace Prize in 1926.

Cavell, Edith Louisa (1865-1915), British nurse. Was in charge of a hospital in Brussels (Belgium) in 1915 when German troops occupied the city; she helped 200 Allied soldiers to escape across the border to Holland. When the Germans arrested her, she admitted what she had done, and was executed by a firing squad.

Churchill, Sir Winston Leonard Spencer (1874-1965), British First Lord of the Admiralty in World War One. The attack at Gallipoli was his idea and when it failed he resigned, but, in 1917, became Minister of Munitions. During the 20's and 30's, he was out of office and out of political favour but in 1940 he became Prime Minister, steering his country through the years of defeat to victory in 1945. The Labour Party won the election in that year but in 1951, at the age of 77, Churchill became Prime Minister for the second time.

Clemenceau, Georges (1841-1929), Prime Minister of France, 1906-9 and 1917-20. He was a great speaker and an aggressive politician, nicknamed "The Tiger". He presided at the Peace Conference in 1919.

Enver Pasha (1881-1922), leader of the Young Turks, whom he joined while he was in the Turkish Army. He made himself Minister of War in 1914, becoming more and more powerful as the war went on. In 1915, he conducted a disastrous offensive on the Russo-Turkish border. When Turkey collapsed, he fled first to Germany and then to Russia.

Foch, Ferdinand (1851-1929), French marshal. Proved himself a skilled strategist in battles on the Western Front (e.g. the Marne, 1914) and in 1918 became C.-in-C. of all the Allied armies on the Western Front. Under his direction, the great final German offensive was checked and turned at the Marne in 1918, and he followed this with the Allied offensives that led to victory.

Fokker, Anthony Hermann Gerard (1890-1939), Dutch pilot and aeroplane builder. By 1913, he owned two aeroplane factories in Germany and during the war he supplied the German army with Fokker biplanes and triplanes. After the war, he established other factories in the U.S., in Holland and in Spain.

George V (1865-1936), King of England, friend and supporter of Haig during the war. He spoke out against the clamour to "Hang the Kaiser" (*cf* Wilhelm II) after the war.

Haig, Douglas (1861-1928), Field Marshal, C.-in-C. of British forces on the Western Front from 1915. To some, he seemed to be insensitive to casualties; to others, he was a dedicated professional soldier who stuck tenaciously to the task of defeating Germany in a war of attrition.

Hindenburg, Paul von Beneckendorff und von (1847-1934), German general who retired in 1911 and was recalled for World War One. With Ludendorff (*cf* below), won victories over the Russians at Tannenberg and Masurian Lakes (1914) at the age of 67. Moved to the Western Front with Ludendorff in 1916 and they were in charge of Germany's last offensives in 1918. Hindenburg was a national hero after the war and became President of the new republic in 1925-34.

Haig   Hindenburg

Jellicoe, John Rushworth, 1st Earl (1859-1935), British admiral. After an active and heroic career starting as a naval cadet, Jellicoe became Third Sea Lord in 1908, and at the war's start he was made C.-in-C. of the Grand Fleet. At the battle of Jutland in 1916, he was not prepared to run the risk of losing the war in order to destroy the German Fleet and, afterwards, he was heavily criticized and relieved of his command, being made First Sea Lord. Yet he was awarded the Order of Merit and later both Houses of Parliament voted their thanks to him; he was also granted £50,000.

Joffre, Joseph Jacques Césaire (1852-1931), French C.-in-C. 1914-16; said to have saved Paris in 1914; a gifted soldier who aroused jealousy of other generals. Replaced by Nivelle and made Marshal of France.

Kerensky, Alexander (1881-1970), a Socialist, took a leading part in the Russian Revolution of 1917 and became Premier of Russia in July. When the Communists took over in the "October Revolution" in November 1917, he fled to France. In 1940 he went to the U.S., and died there.

Kitchener, Horatio Herbert, 1st Earl Kitchener of Khartoum (1850-1916), victor for Britain at Omdurman in 1898, was made Secretary of State for War in August 1914. Won great praise for the way he built up the British Army. Drowned on his way to Russia when HMS *Hampshire* struck a mine.

Lenin, Vladimir Ilyich (1870-1924), who changed his surname from Ulyanov, was a Marxist revolutionary from his student days. In 1905, he took a leading part in a revolt and afterwards had to live abroad. He settled in Switzerland and from there returned to Russia after the February revolution of 1917. When the Communists seized power in November, Lenin became Chairman of the Council of People's Commissars (Prime Minister) and, within two weeks, he asked Germany for peace. Throughout the civil war of 1918-21, Lenin retained power in the face of constant opposition. He died of brain disease and his body lies in a mausoleum in Red Square, Moscow.

Lloyd George, David, Ist Earl of Dwyfor (1863-1945), Prime Minister of Britain, 1916-22. He made his name as a dynamic Liberal politician and after becoming Minister of Munitions and Secretary of State for War, he replaced Asquith as Premier. Known as "the man who won the war", he played a leading role in the Peace Settlement, but at home he lost support and never held office after 1922.

Ludendorff, Erich von (1865-1937), German general, won battles of Tannenberg and Masurian Lakes on Eastern Front, 1914. He worked with Hindenburg (*cf* above) because he was considered too young to command alone. After their success against Russia, they were moved to the Western Front in 1916 and directed Germany's final offensives in 1918.

Lloyd George   Ludendorff

Mackensen, A.L.F. August von (1849-1945), German Field-Marshal. Fought in the Franco-Prussian war. At the start of the First World War, he commanded the 9th Army on the Eastern Front, with several victories against the Russians. In 1916, his army overran Serbia, and invaded Rumania.

Mannerheim, Carl Gustav Emil, Baron (1867-1951), Finnish soldier and statesman, joined the Russian Army in 1889 and was a general on the Eastern Front in World War One. After the Russian revolution, Finland became an independent country and Mannerheim went home to raise an army to fight the Communists. He drove back the Communist forces with the aid of 9,000 Germans in early 1918. Mannerheim retired in 1919 but in 1939-40 Finland was again threatened by Russia and he returned to command the Finnish forces. He was C-in-C 1939-44 and President of Finland 1944-6.

Nicholas II, Tsar (1868-1918), succeeded to the throne of Imperial Russia in 1894. By nature well-intentioned, he proved to be a deplorable ruler, forever wavering between half-hearted reforms and old-fashioned tyranny. During the war, he foolishly took over command of Russia's armies, allowing home affairs to be mis-managed by the Tsarina, who herself was dominated by a sinister monk named Rasputin (*cf* below). In 1918, the Tsar and his family were put to death by their Communist guards.

Nivelle, Robert Georges (1856-1924), French general. Made his name in October-December 1916 when he recaptured forts in the Verdun area. He was made C.-in-C. in December 1916 but in May 1917 his offensive at Aisne failed and he was superseded by Pétain (*cf* below).

Pershing, General John Joseph (1860-1948), commander of the U.S. Expeditionary Force to Europe in 1917, having commanded an expedition to Mexico against Francisco Villa in 1916. He directed the first entirely U.S. operation of the war in Europe in 1918, and in 1919, Congress recreated and gave to Pershing the rank of General of the Armies, held previously only by Washington.

Pétain, Henri Philippe Omer, Marshal of France (1856-1951), took over command in the Battle of Verdun, 1916, and became a national hero. In 1917 became C.-in-C. of the French Army. In post-war years, he supported the Maginot Line which was by-passed by the Germans in World War Two. When France was overrun in 1940, Pétain became Prime Minister and made peace with the Germans. At the end of the war, he was tried for treason and sentenced to death. The sentence was changed to life imprisonment and he died in prison.

Pershing   Pétain

Poincaré, Raymond (1860-1934), French statesman, President of France 1913-20, he was also three times Prime Minister before and after the war.

Rasputin, Gregory Efimovitch (1871-1916), Russian monk who from 1907 had influence over Tsar Nicholas II (*cf* above) and his wife. He was hated by most Russians, including the nobility, and was murdered by a party of noblemen.

Scheer, Reinhard (1863-1928), German admiral, commanded the German High Seas Fleet 1916-18, was in command at the Battle of Jutland (German: Battle of Skagerrak).

Smuts, Jan Christiaan (1870-1950), South African statesman and field-marshal. Fought in the Boer War and in 1916 led Allied forces against the Germans in German East Africa, leaving in 1917 to represent South Africa at the Imperial War Conference. At the Paris Peace Conference, he became one of the authors of the Covenant of the League of Nations. Prime Minister of South Africa 1919-24 and 1939-48.

Spee, Count Maximilian von (1861-1914), German admiral, in late 1914 commander of the commerce-raiding force in the Pacific Ocean. In battle with a British squadron, he sank two warships. A force was sent to find him and he was brought to battle off the Falkland Islands. Six out of his eight ships were destroyed and von Spee went down with his flagship.

Tirpitz, Alfred von (1849-1930), German admiral. As Secretary of State for the German Navy 1897-1916, he raised a navy to challenge Britain's supremacy on the seas. He was C.-in-C. of the German Navy from August 1914 to March 1916, a ruthless advocate of unrestricted U-boat warfare.

Trotsky, Leon, born Lev Davidovich Bronstein (1879-1940), a Russian-Jewish revolutionary. After the rising in 1905, Trotsky lived abroad until returning to Russia in 1917. In the civil war of 1918-21, he raised an army of five million men for the Communists, but was forced into exile by Stalin, and was murdered by a Communist agent in Mexico.

Wilhelm II (1859-1941), Emperor of Germany 1888-1918, who personified the German generals' desire for military glory and colonies. Having sacked Bismarck early in his reign, he supported von Tirpitz's plan for a navy to match Britain's and encouraged Austria-Hungary in her demands against Serbia. But he tried to draw back when he saw a world war was going to occur. During the war, he was only a figure-head, but was obliged to abdicate in November 1918. He died in exile in Holland.

Wilson, Thomas Woodrow (1856-1924), President of the United States 1913-21. Preserved U.S. neutrality until Germany declared unrestricted U-boat warfare in 1917 and began sinking U.S. ships. Early in 1918, produced a 14-point peace plan which encouraged Germany to ask for an armistice. Was largely responsible for the establishment of the League of Nations and bitterly disappointed when Congress refused to allow the U.S. to become a member.

Wilhelm II   Wilson

Fighter Aces

The Aces
World War One was the first war in which aeroplanes were used. Once fighter aircraft had been developed, specialist fighter pilots appeared, soon to be known as "aces." The French called a pilot an ace when he had shot down five enemy aircraft, and the first ace was Roland Garros. But Garros' career soon ended: he force-landed on a bombing raid in 1915 and was taken prisoner.

A German ace was called an *oberkanone* (top gun) and he obtained the title when he had shot down ten enemy aircraft. On entering the war, the United States adopted the ace system, awarding the title for five enemy aircraft shot down. But Britain did not use the system. True, the most successful British pilots became known as aces, but this did not happen automatically when they had shot down a certain number of enemy aircraft.

The Red Knight
The French and the Germans gave widespread publicity to their aces and they became the romantic heroes of an otherwise bloody and degrading struggle. The greatest of them all was the German Rittmeister (Cavalry Captain) Manfred von Richthofen, known as the "Red Knight" because he flew in a red aeroplane. Richthofen scored 80 victories before he was shot down on April 21, 1918, by Captain Roy Brown, a Canadian in the RAF.

Richthofen was flying a Fokker Dr1 and was on the tail of a Young Australian, Lt. W. R. May, when Brown dived down and opened fire. The red triplane sank to earth and made an almost perfect landing in No Man's Land. The engine ticked for a few moments, then stopped.

In the trenches close by was a group of Australian soldiers, and one of them called to the pilot to come out, but no-one climbed out of the plane.

An Australian crawled through the barbed wire and tied a rope to the undercarriage and the Aussies pulled the Fokker to a place sheltered from enemy fire.

There they looked into the cockpit and found the greatest fighter pilot of World War One sitting bolt upright with blood around his mouth. He was dead. A single bullet had pierced his chest.

The "Eagle of Lille"
The first German fighter ace was Lt. Max Immelmann, the "Eagle of Lille." He scored his first victory on August 1, 1915 in one of the new Fokker E 1's—the first fighter plane able to fire its machine-gun straight ahead. Before he was shot down in flames himself on June 18, 1916, Immelmann sent down 15 Allied aircraft.

He also invented the "Immelmann turn," used by fighter pilots on both sides. In this manoeuvre, Immelmann allowed an enemy pilot to close in on him from the rear and then soared upwards in what looked like a loop. At the top of the loop, he suddenly pulled out and, all too often, his pursuer went on the loop, losing sight of Immelmann. At this point, Immelmann would be turning to come in behind him, spandau machine-guns blazing. It was the fighter pilot's ideal position for the kill.

"A brave and chivalrous foeman"
Immelmann was taught his trade by the father-figure of German combat fighting, Hauptmann Oswald Boelcke. Apart from scoring 40 victories, Boelcke became famous as an ideal leader of a squadron. He spent a great deal of time instructing his pilots. Boelcke was killed in an air accident on October 28, 1916.

A British plane flew over the graveyard at Cambrai when he was being buried and dropped a wreath bearing the inscription, "To the memory of Captain Boelcke, a brave and chivalrous foeman. From the men of the Royal Flying Corps." Two years later, when Richthofen died, even the knights

△ **Left to right:** Oswald Boelcke, the greatest figure in the early German air force; Max Immelmann, his pupil; Manfred von Richthofen, who painted his aeroplanes blood-red.

△ **Left to right:** "Billy" Bishop, "Mick" Mannock, James McCudden: British fighter aces.

of the skies were becoming disillusioned with the war.

The French Aces
France's top ace, Capitaine René Fonck, was the greatest Allied fighter pilot of World War One. Some say that, in technical skill, he was a greater pilot than von Richthofen. He started his career in July 1916 by fitting a machine-gun to his plane, and within a few months had shot down five enemy aircraft.

He often sent an aircraft down with only five or six shots instead of long bursts of fire; the shots were placed, in his own words, "comme avec la main"—"as if by hand." He continued as a combat pilot to the end of the war, scoring his 75th victory on November 1, 1918.

Capitaine Georges Guynemer shot down fewer aircraft than Fonck—54. Yet he was France's most popular fighter pilot. He shot down his first enemy on July 19, 1915 and for the next 14 months, France thrilled to his exploits. Seven times he was shot down and seven times he escaped alive. Never in good health, he seemed to be growing sick but he would not give up flying and, on September 11, 1917, he failed to return from a patrol. All France mourned for him. Neither his body nor his aircraft was ever found.

The British Aces
Britain's first fighter ace was Captain Albert Ball, only 20 years old. Stories of his fearless charges at enemy aircraft, whatever their number, were soon

being told at home. In less than a year, he shot down 44 enemy aircraft, usually flying a Nieuport Scout, and coming up underneath his victim. He crashed behind enemy lines on May 7, 1917. No one ever found out what caused him to crash.

Britain's top ace was Major Edward "Mick" Mannock who is officially credited with 73 victories. Mannock was known to pass credit for many a victory to newcomers in his squadron, and the true total of his victims is unknown.

Like Boelcke, he had the complete trust of his pilots and one of them wrote, "Flying with Mannock is as safe as lying in bed. His leadership is foolproof."

On July 26, 1918, a random shot from the ground hit Mannock's petrol tank and he went down in flames behind enemy lines. His grave has never been found. Hardly anyone in England heard of his exploits in his lifetime and he was awarded the Victoria Cross nearly a year after his death.

Other top aces (and number of victories)

Lt Charles Nungesser (French)	45
Capt. Edward Rickenbacker (American)	26
Second Lt. Frank Luke, Jnr. (American)	21
Major J. T. B. McCudden (British)	57
Lt.-Col. W. A. Bishop (British)	72
Maggiore Francesco Baracea (Italian)	34
Staff Capt. A. A. Kazakov (Russian)	17
Second Lt. Willy Coppens (Belgian)	37
Oberleutnant Ernst Udet (German)	62
Hauptmann Godwin Brumowski (Austro-Hungarian)	40

Peace Talks

The Armistice Terms
By the terms of the Armistice signed at 5 a.m. on November 11, 1918, in a railway carriage shunted into a siding in the Forest of Compiègne, the Germans agreed to the following:

1 The immediate evacuation by Germany of all occupied countries.
2 The return of all prisoners of war.
3 The return to France of the provinces of Alsace and Lorraine (taken by Germany in the Franco-Prussian war of 1870-1).
4 The evacuation by the Germans of the west bank of the River Rhine.
5 The surrender of 5,000 guns, 30,000 machine-guns and 2,000 aeroplanes.
6 The surrender of 5,000 locomotives, 150,000 railway wagons and 5,000 motor lorries.
7 The surrender of six battle-cruisers, the best ten battleships, eight light cruisers and the best 50 destroyers.
8 The surrender of all German U-boats.

The Peace of Paris, 1919
Three men dominated the talks in the Peace of Paris. They were President Wilson of the United States, David Lloyd George, Prime Minister of Britain, and Georges Clemenceau, Premier of France.

Italy, Japan and the smaller nations that had fought on the side of the Allies were also represented but Germany, Austria, Bulgaria and Turkey had no representatives present. The peace was to be dictated solely by the Allies. Russia was not represented because the country was in the grip of a civil war and she had negotiated peace with Germany in 1918.

President Wilson put forward one idea: "We are not enemies of the German people." But the French had a different viewpoint. Their country had been invaded by Germany twice in a century—in 1870 and in 1914. They wanted to push their border eastwards to the Rhine as a protection against any future attack.

The other Allies would not agree to this, but Britain and the United States agreed that if, at a future date, Germany again invaded France, they would come to her assistance. (The U.S. Congress never ratified this agreement.) When Marshal Foch heard of this he said, prophetically, "This is not peace. It is an armistice for twenty years."

The Terms of the Peace of Paris
By the Peace, the following changes took place:

1 Alsace and Lorraine were given back to France.
2 The border of Belgium was adjusted giving her slightly more territory.
3 Poland was formed into an independent nation with a strip of land through East Prussia to the port of Danzig.
4 Finland, Estonia, Latvia and Lithuania became independent states, and so did Austria, Hungary and the new countries of Czechoslovakia and Yugoslavia (including Serbia, Montenegro and parts of Austria, Hungary and Bulgaria).
5 German colonies were made into mandates of the countries that conquered them, being looked after on behalf of the League of Nations.
6 The peace treaty included the formation of the League of Nations as had been proposed by President Wilson.

7 Germany had to hand over the coalmines of the Saar to France for 15 years. Then there was to be a vote among the people of the region to see whether they wanted to remain under the French.
8 Germany had to disband her army although she was allowed to retain a force of 100,000 men for use inside Germany. She had to destroy all military weapons, and was forbidden to make tanks, artillery or military aircraft. Most of her navy had to be surrendered.
9 The peace treaty signed by Germany, the Treaty of Versailles, declared that Germany was responsible for World War One.
10 The Germans had to pay £6,600 million in reparation to injured nations and the first instalment was fixed as £20 million to be paid by the end of May 1921.

What the war cost Germany
This is what the Treaty of Versailles did to Germany:

1 Reduced her size by one eighth and her population by 6½ million.
2 Took away all her colonies and overseas investments, one sixth of her farmland, one-eighth of her livestock, one-tenth of her factories. Reduced her merchant fleet, crippled her navy, limited her army to about the size of Belgium's and this for internal use only.
3 Nevertheless, the Treaty of Versailles was not a vindictive settlement, considering the nature of the war. Germany was not crushed or dismembered, and she never paid the reparations in full. However, it did humiliate the Germans, who bitterly resented the "war guilt" clause.

The League of Nations

President Wilson's plan for the League
The idea for the League of Nations was put forward by President Wilson among his 14 points for peace, and the covenant (set of rules) of the League of Nations was included in each of the treaties signed in the Peace of Paris—the Treaty of St Germain with Austria, the Treaty of Neuilly with Bulgaria, the Treaty of Trianon with the Hungarians, the Treaty of Sèvres with the Turks and the Treaty of Versailles with Germany.

Each treaty gave the responsibility for enforcing its provisions to the League of Nations.

The League came into being on January 10, 1920, with its headquarters in the Palace of Nations in Geneva, Switzerland.

The aims of the League were to promote international co-operation and to maintain international peace and security. The League suffered an early blow when the United States refused to join. Upon his return from the peace conference, President Wilson presented the covenant to Congress and found that it was not accepted. Ultimately, the U.S. made a separate peace with Germany.

Wilson suffered a stroke in 1920 that paralyzed him and he did not seek re-election as President. His party supported the League of Nations, but their rivals won the election. Afterwards, the U.S., under President Warren Harding, had little to do with affairs in Europe.

The League of Nations was not a success. It was officially disbanded in 1946 after World War Two and the United Nations took its place.

The Members of the League of Nations
This list shows the original members of the League of Nations. Many other nations joined later and many withdrew from the League before it was disbanded in 1946.

Argentina	Italy
Australia	Japan
Belgium	Liberia
Bolivia	Netherlands
Brazil	New Zealand
Canada	Nicaragua
Chile	Norway
Colombia	Panama
Cuba	Paraguay
Czechoslovakia	Peru
Denmark	Poland
El Salvador	Romania
France	South Africa
Great Britain	Spain
Greece	Sweden
Guatemala	Switzerland
Haiti	Thailand
Honduras	Uruguay
India	Venezuela
Iran	Yugoslavia

The Two Sides

The opponents in World War One were as follows:

The Allies
Belgium	Japan
Brazil	Liberia
British Empire	Montenegro
China	Nicaragua
Costa Rica	Panama
Cuba	Portugal
France	Romania
Greece	Russia
Guatemala	San Marino
Haiti	Serbia
Honduras	Siam
Italy	United States

The Central Powers
Austria-Hungary	Germany
Bulgaria	Ottoman Empire

Fighters versus Bombers

Wargames duplicate the action of real or imaginary battles on a miniature scale. The battlefield in this case is a map, drawn to suitable scale, of the combat area.

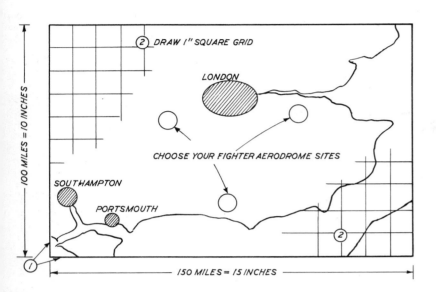

By following the plans, you can create a battle between fighters and Zeppelins.

A suitable scale for a map covering World War I bombing attacks on London is 10 miles = 1in. You can copy a 40 miles = 1in (1:2,500,000) map, which is a common size to be found in most atlases. The wargame map will be 4 times bigger.

Start by drawing a rectangle 15ins wide and 10 ins deep on a piece of suitable paper (see left: 1). On this, draw a grid of 1in squares lightly in pencil (2). If a ¼in grid is then drawn on your 1:2,500,000 scale atlas map it will be easy to copy the outlines required onto the wargame map. Then mark the position of the main towns, as shown, and chose suitable sites for the fighter aerodromes.

Pin the map down onto a flat board, or stick to a piece of thick, flat card (rigid corrugated packing case card is ideal for this purpose).

Bomber range scale

▷ A range scale is made for each type of bomber to be used, as shown on the right. The scale is a length of ½in × ⅛in hardwood strip, marked off in an **hours** scale. These divisions represent the **distance** the bomber can cover in these times, to the same scale as that of the map. To work out the required divisions, use the following table:

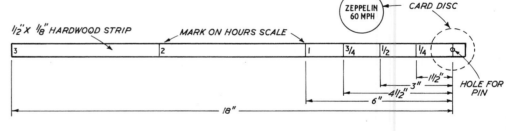

Aircraft speed (mph)	Scale distance for			
	¼hr	½hr	¾hr	1hr
50	1¼ins	2½ins	3¾ins	5ins
60	1½ins	3ins	4½ins	6ins
70	1¾ins	3½ins	5¼ins	7ins
80	2ins	4ins	6ins	8ins
90	2¼ins	4½ins	6¾ins	9ins
100	2½ins	5ins	7½ins	10ins
110	2¾ins	5½ins	8¼ins	11ins
120	3ins	6ins	9ins	12ins

The diagram shows a bomber scale made out for a 1914-1916 era Zeppelin having a cruising speed of 60mph. Complete the scale by drilling a hole at the starting point of the scale to take a pin, and add a disc of card on which is marked the name of the bomber (ie Zeppelin in this case). Make scales for all the bomber types you intend to use in the game.

Fighter range scale

▷ This is made in a similar way to the bomber scale, marked out in hour divisions according to the speed of the fighter. Note, however, that the speed to use is the "climb-to-intercept" speed of the fighter, not the maximum speed. The diagram shows the scale plotted for a Bristol Scout (maximum speed 90mph, but "climb-to-intercept" speed 45mph). Since "45mph" does not appear in the table on the left, work to half the 90mph measurements.

Note that the **length** of the fighter scale is limited by the **endurance** of the aircraft concerned. The endurance, in hours, represents the extreme range, ie the maximum length of scale. For the aircraft to

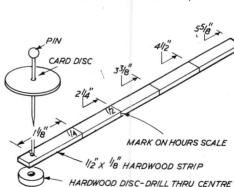

return to the same aerodrome, the length of the scale is **one half** of the endurance time.

A range scale should be made for each of the fighter aircraft types to be used.

British fighters

Performance figures for British fighters of the earlier war period are given. You can find others by further readings. Note that

the important figures for making a Fighter Range Scale are "climb-to-intercept" speed (shown as "Climb" in table), and endurance.

	DH2	FE8	Bristol Scout	Sopwith Pup	Sopwith Camel
speed (mph)	90	95	90	110	110
climb (mph*)	45	45	45	90	95
endurance (hrs)	2¾	4	2½	3	2½
ceiling (ft)	14,500	14,500	15,500	17,500	19,000

*In the absence of any other information, take this as one half the maximum speed.

Wargame: Zeppelins attack London

1 Enemy spotted!

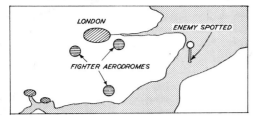

Decide the point on your map at which the enemy is first spotted. To make the wargame easier to illustrate we will pick a point off the Kent coast of England, as shown. (An alert lookout on a warship could have spotted the Zeppelins and radioed a warning back).

2 Identify type and number

The warning has been received—Zeppelins heading in the direction of London. The appropriate Bomber range stick is selected (Zeppelin) and pinned on the point reported.

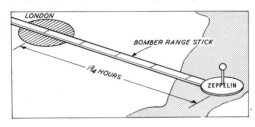

Line the range stick up with London, as shown. You can now read off the time taken for the Zeppelins to reach London if they hold their expected course and speed—eg 1¼ hrs.

3 Alert fighter aerodromes

Each fighter aerodrome has its squadron of fighter aircraft at the ready. For each aerodrome you need a Fighter range stick.*

The decision is made to alert Aerodrome A which has Bristol Scouts. Take a Scout range stick and pin to the centre of aerodrome A.

4 Lay off the intercept

Swing the fighter range stick round until it crosses the bomber range stick *at the same point on the two time scales.*

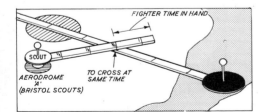

This shows the course and time taken to intercept, with the fighters taking off immediately. The fighter range stick should overlap the bomber range stick, and the length of the overlap shows the "time in hand" fighters will have to engage the enemy, assuming they meet at the planned intercept.

5 Plan the strategy

See if there may be better ways of dealing with the situation. To give the fighters more time in hand for engagement after intercept, swing the fighter range stick to give a shorter course (and time) to intercept. This will also delay the take-off *by the difference in the two times* on the fighter and bomber scale where they cross.

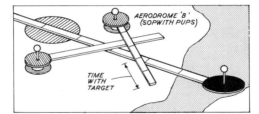

Perhaps this will mean that the enemy is being allowed to get too near to London before being intercepted. See if an earlier intercept is possible, even if this does mean that the fighters will not have enough endurance to get back to their own aerodrome.

6 Call up another squadron?

Aerodrome 'B' has Sopwith Pups on station—faster than the Bristol Scouts, too. Plot an intercept with these fighters from this second aerodrome.

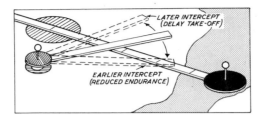

What is best now? The Pups will get to an intercept first, according to the plot. Or would you prefer to hold the Pups back so that they can intercept at the same time, and position, as the Scouts from aerodrome 'A'?

7 Success or failure?

It is one thing to plot intercepts, but quite another for the fighter pilots to find the enemy in the sky—and then successfully shoot them down. You have to decide what the chances are. See if you can find facts and figures which give an idea of the chances.

To take into account this question of "chance" you can throw a dice, scoring like this, say:

6 – enemy shot down;
5 – enemy intercepted, badly damaged;
4 – enemy intercepted, slightly damaged.
Any throw less than 4 counts as failure to intercept. Repeat the throws for each of the Zeppelins mounting the attack.

8 Intercept on the return?

What if the enemy has got through? Is there a chance to make an intercept on his return journey? The fighters from aerodromes 'A' and 'B' will have used up all their endurance by this time, so call up aerodrome 'C'.

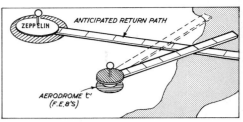

This aerodrome has FE 8s—slow, but with a good endurance. Provided they are alerted in time they should be able to make an intercept before, or by the coast. Remember, however, they must be left enough endurance to get back to land, so plan the intercept to take place as far inland as possible.

9 Finally, write up the log

Write up a log of action taken and results achieved. Probably there are lessons to be learnt already. For example, it might be better to have the Sopwith Pups at aerodrome 'A' rather than 'B'. Perhaps also some better aerodromes can be found for fighter defence of London? And, of course, you can always ask for some faster fighters!

Varying the attack

The wargame strategy can be more interesting by varying the attack—like Zeppelins attacking in one line and Gotha bombers on another course. Two people can take part.

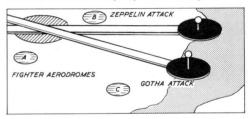

Follow the same stages through, plotting intercept to the best advantage with the available fighter aircraft. After a few raids like this both fighter and bomber commands will have learnt a lot of lessons—and probably want to change their strategies!

One course for the bombers to follow is to try to fool the fighter command as to where the attack is being directed.

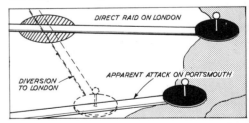

Here is one type of diversionary attack. One force of bombers sets out on a direct attack on London. Another heads, apparently, for Portsmouth. Once the main fighter force has concentrated on defending the capital, the second bomber group diverts to London—to arrive as the remaining fighters are running out of endurance! Once caught out in this way, fighter command will have learnt to hold some aircraft back in reserve.

German bombers

During the early years of the war the Zeppelin was the only German bomber with a range great enough to reach London (and beyond) and return to Germany. Speed was about 60mph and ceiling 15,000 feet. By 1918 Zeppelin design had improved, with speed rising to 80mph and ceiling to 20,000 feet.

The Gotha bomber came into service in 1917 with a cruising speed of 70mph at 12,000 feet. In selecting your bomber types (you can look up details of others in reference books on World War I aircraft), remember to select fighters of the same period to oppose them. (The Sopwith Snipe, for example, did not appear in service until mid-1918).

---

* Note: aircraft *ceiling* should also be taken into account in a wargame. If bombers are attacking at an altitude of 17,000 feet, say, it will be no good sending fighters to intercept if their ceiling is lower than this figure.

Poems and Songs of the War

Among the legacies of World War One are songs and poems that convey to some extent the feelings of people caught up in the throes of the greatest international struggle in history.

Many of the songs were sung on the march. They reflect a brave cheerfulness—" Pack up your troubles in your old kitbag/ And smile, smile, smile." Some express the sentiments of young lovers being separated— " Smile awhile and kiss me sad adieu . . ." These were published songs—known, played and sung at home as well as at the front.

There were also poems made up by the soldiers, and these were hardly ever bitter.

The bitterness and disillusionment came in the poems written by true poets who found themselves in uniform. Charles Sorley was the first poet to try to express the futility of war. He wrote:
" When you see millions of mouthless dead
Across your dream in pale battalions go
Say not soft things as other men have said . . ."

△ **Wilfred Owen** (1893-1918) emerged as the greatest of the British war poets. A young officer, he was killed on the Western Front. His poetry conveyed with disturbing clarity the ugliness and outrage of war. By contrast, the work of Britain's first great war poet, Rupert Brooke (1887-1915), shows war as a brave adventure for young heroes. Brooke never served in the trenches. A sub-lieutenant in the Royal Naval Division, he died from illness on the way to Gallipoli.

△ **Drawing of himself as an artillery-man by the French war poet, Apollinaire** (1880-1918). Apollinaire was already a well-known poet at the war's start, famous for writing a new type of poetry that broke away from old traditions. He enlisted as a private and soon became an officer. He bombarded his old friends with letters and postcards in verse from the battlefront. Wounded in 1916, he was sent home and lived out the war in Paris. His poetry held up a mirror to the scenes of the war, but it did not reflect the underlying feelings of embattling humanity as Owen, Robert Graves and Siegfried Sassoon sought to do.

Anthem for Doomed Youth

What passing-bells for those who died as cattle?
  Only the monstrous anger of the guns.
  Only the stuttering rifles' rapid rattle
Can patter out their hasty orisons.
No mockeries for them from prayers or bells,
  Nor any voice of mourning save the choirs,—
The shrill, demented choirs of wailing shells;
  And bugles calling for them from sad shires.

What candles may be held to speed them all?
  Not in the hands of boys, but in their eyes
Shall shine the holy glimmer of good-byes.
  The pallor of girls' bows shall be their pall;
Their flowers the tenderness of patient minds,
And each slow dusk a drawing-down of blinds.

Wilfred Owen

(By kind permission of Mr Harold Owen and Chatto and Windus Ltd)

from Nocturnal Landscape

Death slaughters them, and they lie under weeds, heavy, fossil, with hands
            full of spiders, mouths scabbed red and brown,
Eyes full of uttermost sleep, the circlet of shadow around their brows,
            blue, waxen, decaying in the smoke of the night
Which sank down, threw shadows far, which spread its vault from hill
            to hill, over forests and rottenness, over brains full of
            dreams, over the hundred dead none carried away,
Over the mass of fire, over laughter and madness, over crosses in fields,
            over pain and despair, over rubble and ash, over the
            river and the ruined town . . .

Anton Schnack 1920

(Translation from the German © Christopher Middleton 1962)

△ **This is the bitter reality of war** that the later war poets strove to put down in words. At Passchendaele in 1917, Haig's chief-of-staff burst into tears as his car struggled through the mud. "Good God," he cried. "Did we really send men to fight in that?"

△ **A song sheet from the war.** This song was sung by soldiers of the Allied armies on the march.

There's a long, long trail a'winding
Into the land of my dreams
Where the nightingales are singing
And a white moon beams
There's a long, long time a'waiting
Till my dreams come true
Till that day I'll be going
Down that long, long trail with you.
(Song)

△ **To the soldier on the march** or in the trenches, the war seemed endless, and home an almost forgotten dream.

Hush! Here comes a Whizz-bang
(Tune: "Hush! Here comes the Dream Man")

Hush! Here comes a Whizz-bang,
Hush! Here comes a Whizz-bang,
Now you soldiers, get down those
stairs,
Down in your dug-outs and say your
prayers,
Hush! Here comes a Whizz-bang,
And it's making straight for you:
And you'll see all the wonders of
No Man's Land
If a Whizz-bang (bump!) hits you.

△ **Sung to the tune of a pre-1914 pantomime song.** Many songs were imitations or parodies of current popular songs.

Oh, see him in the House of Commons,
Passing laws to put down crime,
While the victims of his passions
Trudge on in mud and slime.
(Song)

△ **A bitter song** expressing contempt for politicians, who, the soldier feels, were responsible for the miseries of the war, and especially for the fighting in the trenches.

Far, Far from Ypres

Far, far from Ypres I long to be,
Where German snipers can't snipe at
me,
Damp is my dug-out,
Cold are my feet,
Waiting for whizz-bangs
To send me to sleep.
(Song)

△ **This song is in a more serious tone,** but parodies a pre-1914 sentimental song. "Ypres" was pronounced "Wypers" at the start of the war by the British soldiers. A "whizz-bang" was the slang term for a light shell fired from one of the smaller field artillery guns. It made a whizzing noise as it flew through the air. Often it exploded as soon as or even before anyone heard it coming.

Index

Note: Numbers in bold refer to illustrations

Further Reading

Available in the United States and Canada:

AMERICAN HERITAGE. *American Heritage History of World War I.* American Heritage 1964.

BALDWIN, HANSON W. *World War I: An Outline History.* Harper & Row 1962.

CHURCHILL, WINSTON S. *The World Crisis.* Scribner's 1963.

COFFMAN, EDWARD M. *The War to End All Wars; The American Military Experience in World War I.* Oxford 1968.

CRUTTWELL, CHARLES R. M. F. *A History of the Great War, 1914-1918.* 2d. ed. Oxford 1936.

FALLS, CYRIL. *The Great War 1914-1918.* Putnam 1961.

FAY, SIDNEY BRADSHAW. *The Origins of the World War.* 2d. ed. rev. Macmillan 1938.

FLEMING, D. F. *The Origins and Legacies of World War I.* Doubleday 1968.

FONCK, RENÉ. *Ace of Aces.* Doubleday 1967.

FREIDEL, FRANK B. *Over There: The Story of America's First Great Overseas Crusade.* Little 1964.

HEMINGWAY, ERNEST. *A Farewell to Arms.* Scribner's 1953.

HOYT, EDWIN P. *The Phantom Raider.* Crowell 1969.

LAWRENCE, T. E. *Seven Pillars of Wisdom: True Story of the Legendary Lawrence of Arabia.* Doubleday 1966.

LIDDELL HART, B. H. *The Real War, 1914-1918.* Little 1964.

PARKINSON, ROGER. *The Origins of World War One.* Putnam 1970.

REMARQUE, ERICH MARIA. *All Quiet on the Western Front.* Little 1929.

REYNOLDS, QUENTIN. *They Fought for the Sky: The Dramatic Story of the First War in the Air.* Holt 1957.

RICKENBACKER, EDWARD V. *Fighting the Flying Circus.* Doubleday 1965.

SNYDER, LOUIS LEO. *Historic Documents of World War I.* Van Nostrand 1958.

STALLINGS, LAURENCE. *The Story of the Doughboys: The AEF in World War I.* Harper & Row 1966.

THOMAS, LOWELL. *With Lawrence in Arabia.* Doubleday 1967.

TUCHMAN, BARBARA W. *The Guns of August.* Macmillan 1962.
        The Zimmermann Telegram. Macmillan 1966.

Available in Britain:

BARBARY, J. *Lawrence and his Desert Raiders.* Parrish 1965.

BENNETT, GEOFFREY. *Naval Battles of the First World War.* Batsford 1968.

BORER, MARY CATHCART. *The First World War.* Macmillan 1970.

DUPUY, T. N. *Campaigns in Southern Europe. Campaigns on the Turkish Fronts. Naval and Overseas War 1914-15. Naval and Overseas War 1916-18. 1918: Decision in the West. 1918: The German Offensives. 1914: The Battles in the East. 1914: The Battles in the West. Stalemate in the Trenches: November 1914—March 1918. Summation: Strategic and Combat Leadership. Triumphs and Tragedies in the East 1915-17. The War in the Air.* All Watts 1967.

FALLS, C. *The First World War.* Longman 1960.

GIBBONS, S. R. AND MORICAN, P. *The League of Nations and UNO.* Longman 1970.

*GRAVES, ROBERT. *Goodbye to All That.* Penguin.

GREY, ELIZABETH. *Friend Within the Gates (Edith Cavell).* Constable 1960.

HOBLEY, L. F. *The First World War.* Blackie 1971.

*JAMES, ROBERT RHODES. *Gallipoli.* Batsford 1965.

*LIDDELL HART, B. H. *A History of the First World War.* Faber 1934.

MACK, DONALD. *Lenin and the Russian Revolution.* Longman 1970.

*REMARQUE, E. M. *All Quiet on the Western Front.* Putnam.

ROBERTS, ELIZABETH MAUCHLINE. *Lenin and the Downfall of Tsarist Russia.* Methuen 1966.

SCOTT-DANIELL, DAVID. *World War One.* Benn 1965.

SELLMAN, R. R. *The First World War.* Methuen.

*SHERRIFF, R. C. *Journey's End.* Heinemann.

SHUKMAN, HAROLD. *Lenin and the Russian Revolution.* Batsford 1967.

*TAYLOR, A. J. P. *The First World War: an illustrated history.* Hamilton 1963.

*TURNER, L. C. F. *The First World War.* Warne 1967. *The Coming of the First World War* Warne 1968.

*More difficult reading.

Acknowledgements

We wish to thank the following individuals and organizations for their assistance and for making available material in their collections.

Key to picture positions:
(T) top (C) centre (L) left (B) bottom (R) right and combinations; for example, (TC) top centre

Bapty *p. 19(TL), 25(BR), 55(C)*
Bibliothèque Nationale, Paris *p. 60(BL)*
Brown Brothers *p. 12(TL)*
Bundesarchiv *p. 6(TL), 54(L)*
Chatto & Windus *p. 60(TL)*
Culver Pictures *p. 38(B)*
Durant, Stewart *p. 42(TR)(BL)(BR), 43(TL)(CR)(B)*
Earl Beatty *cover*
Fotoarchiv, VHU, Prague *p. 46(CR)*
Heeresgeschichtliches Museums *p. 5(BR)*
Hulton Picture Library *p. 6(BL), 13, 21(BC), 49(R), 55(L)*
"L'Illustration" *p. 34(TL), 44(TL)*
Imperial War Museum *p. 6(BC), 8(CL)(TR), 9(TL)(BL), 10(R), 11(T), 12(BR), 16(TR), 22(B), 23(BR), 26(R), 29(L), 33(BL), 37(TL), 38(T), 41(TL), 44(TR)(BL)(BR), 45(CR)(BR), 48(B), 53(L)(C)(R), 54(CL), 55(TR), 56(TL)(TC), 61(T)(B), back cover*
Mansell Collection *p. 34(R), 39(B), 41(BR)*
Military Museum, Belgrade *p. 5(BL)*

Musée de la Guerre, Paris *p. 46(L)*
Musée Royal de L'Armee, Brussels *p. 43(TR), 48(T)*
Museo Storico Italiano/Rovereto *p. 11(CR)*
National Archives *p. 55(C)*
National Portrait Gallery *p. 29(CR)*
Novosti *p. 31(BL), 54(L)*
Odhams Ltd. *p. 49(BL)*
Popperfoto *p. 24(TL), 52(R)*
Princip Museum, Sarajevo *p. 52(L)*
"Punch" *p. 39(TR)*
Smithsonian Institution *p. 36(TL)*
Snark International *p. 11(BR), 49(TL)*
Staatsbibliothek, Berlin *p. 7(CR)(BR), 34(BL)*
Südd-Verlag, Munich *p. 8(TL)(BL), 9(TR), 16(BL), 40(B), 42(TL), 45(TR)*
Ullstein *p. 15(BL), 30(BR), 31(T)*
Viollet, Roger *p. 18(B)*
Wehrgeschichtliches Museum, Rastatt *p. 2-3*

Artists and photographers

Allen, Julian *p. 41(TR)*
Batchelor, John *p. 7(L), 14(BR), 15(T)(B)(C), 16(TL), 17(B), 20(B), 21(T), 24(C), 25(T), 27(T)(C), 31(CL), 32(B), 36(R),*
Beville, Henry *p. 36(TL)*

Dyson, Will *p. 49(BL)*
P.D.A.I. *p. 20(TL), 23(L), 32(T), 50(T)*
Robertson, Alan *p. 12(BL)*
Sarson, Peter *p. 24(BL)*
Spain, Alan *p. 43(TR)*
Wood, Owen *p. 19(R)*
Wyllie, W., RA *cover*

Project author

R. H. Warring *p. 58-59*

Publishers

The Wilfred Owen poem on *p. 60* is from COLLECTED POEMS. Copyright Chatto and Windus Ltd. 1946, © 1963. Reprinted by permission of New Directions Publishing Corporation, New York.

If we have unwittingly infringed copyright in any picture or photograph reproduced in this publication, we tender our sincere apologies and will be glad of the opportunity, upon being satisfied as to the owner's title, to pay an appropriate fee as if we had been able to obtain prior permission.